Arguments for Socialism

Series editor: John Harrison

Arguments for Socialism is a series of popular and provocative books which deal with the economic and political crisis in Britain today. The series argues the need for a radical rethinking of major political questions and contributes to the debates on strategy for the left.

'One of the main reasons why the Tories swept to power in 1979 was that the Labour movement had over the years almost ceased to argue for socialism. This series, *Arguments for Socialism*, can play a significant part in re-establishing the necessity for a socialism that is democratic, libertarian and humane.' *Tony Benn*

Other **Arguments for Socialism**

Take Over the City: The Case for Public Ownership of Financial Institutions Richard Minns

Getting It Together: Women as Trade Unionists
Jenny Beale

More Than We Can Chew: The Crazy World of Food and Farming
Charlie Clutterbuck and Tim Lang

It Makes You Sick: The Politics of the NHS
Colin Thunhurst

Hard Times: The World Economy in Turmoil
Bob Sutcliffe

The Cuts Machine: The Politics of Public Expenditure
David Hall

Due South: Socialists and World Development
Jeremy Hill and Hilary Scannell

Making it Public: Evidence and Action against Privatisation
Dexter Whitfield

Blowing the Whistle: The Politics of Sport
Garry Whannel

Planning is Good for You

The Case for Popular Control

George Blazyca

Pluto Press

First published in 1983 by Pluto Press Limited,
The Works, 105a Torriano Avenue,
London NW5 2RX

British Library Cataloguing in Publication Data
Blazyca, George
Planning is good for you.—(Arguments for socialism)
1. Social policy.
I. Title
361.6'20 HN18
ISBN 0-86104-506-8

Cover designed by Clive Challis A Gr R
Cover photograph: John Sturrock/Network
Computerset by Promenade Graphics Limited
Block 23a Lansdown Industrial Estate, Cheltenham GL51 8PL
Printed and bound in Great Britain
by Richard Clay (The Chaucer Press) Limited, Bungay, Suffolk

To Rachel and Anna

Contents

Acknowledgements

My intellectual debts in writing this book are enormous. Whilst I have tried to point to the authors of particular ideas as the story unfolds, there may still be omissions due to the unconscious nature of 'influence'.

Thanks are due to Pat Knight in the office of the School of Social Sciences at Thames Polytechnic for help in getting parts of a hurriedly scrawled manuscript efficiently typed. I am also very grateful to Wendy Blazyca for taking on enough typing to enable me to meet John Harrison's tight deadlines. Both John Harrison and Richard Kuper gave me enormous help in improving the argument and its flow. Richard Minns was good enough to give me some of his valuable time, and he, Robin Murray and Hilary Wainwright all commented on a draft of chapter five.

While all these people and many others have helped me a great deal, the opinions expressed in this book are mine, and all responsibility for them rests with me.

1.

Why Plan?

Waste and inequality in capitalism

The deficiencies of British capitalism are well known and no more keenly felt in the early 1980s than by the millions of men and women who are currently unemployed. Yet everyone knows that there are jobs that need doing. Unemployment on such a scale is obviously wasteful. It should surely be a simple thing to offer people socially useful work. It should be, but British capitalism finds the task an impossible one, and this is its major shortcoming in the early 1980s. Most people would be prepared to reorganise economic affairs to avoid this waste if they knew how. It is hoped that this book will help identify how such a reorganisation might take place and the main problems likely to confront it.

Apart from unemployment, there are many other things wrong with this creaking, profit-oriented, need-neglecting system. It may have avoided mass unemployment in earlier post-war years but it could not function even then without generating inequality. That was a time when some Labour politicians were busy singing the praises of the new 'mixed economy', a post-capitalist economy, implemented by socially aware entrepreneurs, based in 'soulful' corporations. But a closer look reveals that the system was making some people poor as rapidly as it made others rich. We may only have glimpsed poverty through the eye of television drama on a Wednesday evening but there was no doubting its existence. The full employment capitalism of those years overlooked social needs, fairness and humanity, as much as the mass unemployment capitalism of the 1980s does.

Waste and inequality are as much a part of capitalism as the drive to maximise profits. Traditionally, socialists have argued that we need to organise economic and social life so that social needs can be met, waste avoided and inequality reduced. This calls for an alternative system of decision-making to the one that currently exists. There is nothing religiously inevitable about waste or inequality – they are the slag heaps of capitalism. The real issue before us is to locate the decisions that lead to social waste. Then it becomes possible to call people to account, to challenge their decisions, and to provide alternatives that are in the interest of ordinary people.

Private decisions – social disaster

The aim of socialist planning is to put decision-making in the open and under social control. It does not take much time studying what makes a capitalist economy tick to notice that in it decisions are made in a very private manner. This raises some interesting questions about the nature of Western democracy. Surely, if that democracy was all that it is cracked up to be it would not permit socially harmful decisions to be taken privately time and time again. Yet until there is an outcry over some spectacular issue such as thalidomide, asbestos, the Ford Pinto (more like a bomb than a car) or huge redundancies, crucial decisions are made in a basically undemocratic manner. There is no social audit before, and only exceptionally after, decisions have been made to produce potentially lethal products in perhaps equally deadly working conditions. There is very rarely any social control over the private decisions that throw people out of work.

So part of the continuing deficiency of British capitalism is that its so-called democracy is defective. It cuts off ordinary people from real decision-making power. It is useless to think that something can be done about capitalist waste or inequality without challenging the right a few people have to make private decisions with wide social consequences. We need to open out decision-making so that it does become a genuinely democratic affair, and waste and inequality are avoided. Socialist planning is about establishing popular control over major economic and social decisions. It should be understood as a system of democratic public discussions, centred on finding answers to the questions – how can social needs be identified and best met and how can we build a just and humane society?

But isn't planning discredited?

It is obvious that the interests of ordinary people have not been served well by British capitalism over recent years. Inequalities have grown wider as the Tories have relentlessly thrown more people onto the already lengthy dole queues inherited from Labour. Reduced family incomes have brought great hardship to many people. The loss of jobs entails depression and demoralisation and the welfare state has been unable to cope effectively with the weight of social problems thrown onto its threadbare fabric. Education, housing, health and anti-poverty programmes have been cut just as the list of 'clients' desperately in need of social service help grows longer.

Growing unemployment and public spending cuts are not inevitable. Nor is it by accident that things have turned out this way. The economy is plagued by high unemployment because of deliberate action by the Thatcher government. Decisions to reduce state spending on social services stem from the same source. Such decisions form part of a coherent, if risky, strategy to regenerate British capitalism in one particular style. That way is one which relies on holding down wages growth and tipping the balance in industrial relations firmly in favour of management. Unemployment is the crucial element of the Thatcher approach but the closure of schools, hospitals and old people's homes also plays a part.

It does not have to be like this. What we have in the UK at present is a government promoting the interests it represents. In the case of the Tories those interests are well known. The decisions made by Thatcher, Howe and Joseph are the decisions that would be made if the directors of Beechams, Metal Box or Taylor Woodrow were running the economy. Few people would disagree that the British economy could do with some 'regenerating' but there is much to argue about when it comes to deciding how. The current restructuring (if indeed there is something more than plant closure going on at present) is one carried out by private capital in the interests of private capital. Ordinary people are used merely to bear the brunt of the 'adjustments' taking place. When the Chancellor or managing directors talk about 'painful but alas unavoidable change' we can be sure that the real pain is not felt in 11 Downing Street or in the boardroom.

There *are* alternatives to Thatcherism. The labour movement has developed its own ideas on invigorating the British economy, in which the term 'planning' figures prominently. Indeed the only coherent alternative to Thatcherism is a planned alternative. But, as soon as 'planning' gets bandied about in discussion many people start to get worried, and rightly so. One purpose of this book is to consider those anxieties, the main one being the view that where planning has been tried it has been discredited.

Chapter two looks at the experience of one kind of planning that has a particularly notorious reputation – Soviet-type central planning. Central planning has turned out to be wasteful and horribly undemocratic. The Soviet and East European regimes have, by identifying socialism with *their* planning, poisoned the word socialism and given ammunition to the political right who can talk convincingly about planning as the road to serfdom. We should be able to talk as convincingly of planning as a device which opens up new avenues for a richer democracy than that familiar to us so far. In fact we *can* talk of planning in such a way but only after looking closely at the Soviet Union and Eastern Europe.

This is the aim of chapter two. Apart from asking the obvious questions – why is Soviet type planning wasteful? why is it undemocratic? and so on – it also looks at the tensions produced by traditional planning, which are unlikely to be manageable without drastic and radical system changes in Eastern Europe. The chapter also examines the brief flourishing of a new Polish pluralism and considers what this may have led to in the early 1980s and what it is still likely to lead to in the future.

Subscribers to Thatcherism often proclaim 'there is no alternative'. They dislike being reminded of the planning that has gone on in the UK in the past, that still goes on in many competitor nations and that goes on, on a day-to-day basis, in most large firms. It seems sensible then to look in chapter three at our own planning experience in the UK. How successful has it been? What lessons are there in it for socialists? These are some of the questions addressed.

When planning is mentioned some people suffer Soviet-induced spasms, while others do not even look so far to find what seems to be a good anti-planning case. 'Look at the British nationalised industries and their poor-to-mediocre performance, look at the grossly bureaucratised welfare state' is the common cry. But these are not good arguments against planning. The UK nationalised industries tell us as much about planning as might be discovered from opening the door to any large private corporation. Decisions in publicly owned enterprises are made by small groups, either in government or in head offices, and they are made in private. There is no nationalised industry in the UK which is run by its employees, in which its customers have any real say, and which could therefore tell us something about socialist planning. The only feature of nationalised industries that sets them apart from private firms is that no one in authority seems sure about their aims. Should they make profits or just break even; should they perform a social service or subsidise private industry?

The Thatcher government hopes that incantation of the magic slogan 'privatisation' will make public enterprise disappear and with it the problem we have mentioned. It is also worth noting that there is an important sense in which this policy is ill-named. If, as far as ordinary people are concerned, the decisions of nationalised industries are already made behind closed doors, then privatisation will make no difference to decision-making processes or to social accountability. What will happen, however, is that the ambiguity surrounding nationalised industries' objectives will be removed: they will become straightforward profit-seeking organisations. Privatisation simply regularises the already essentially private manner in which nationalised industries are run in the UK. Socialist planning is about something different. It is concerned with enlarging democracy within public enterprise.

So, too, if we look at the welfare state. The growing hospital waiting lists or the poor quality of state education in some areas do not provide valid arguments either against socialist planning or for the privatisation of some social services, notably health. The main problem with the welfare state has been that working people have never had any particularly good reason to view the welfare state as *theirs*. It has never been clear how ordinary people can shape health and education policy in their communities. How many workers regard hospitals, health centres, schools, colleges and universities as *their* institutions, existing for *their* benefit? Of course the deeper issue is that social services will always be difficult to accommodate in capitalist society. The logics of social need and private profits do not sit comfortably together. This distinction is examined in the last chapter, where an economics of common sense in the interests of working people is developed.

The major experience of national planning in Britain has been during wartime, and then, after the second world war, as the supposedly favourite tool of Labour governments in running the economy. Wartime planning seemed to work reasonably well, though it was not socialist planning, and is looked at in chapter three. The main interest of this chapter is in considering Labour Party planning. Labour governments have never planned successfully. An argument continues between those who say it was due to lack of effort and those who blame lack of technique and ability. In one form or another most of this book is devoted to Labour Party planning and what has gone wrong with it. It argues that the Labour Party must prepare for and counter the resistance and hostility that proposals for socialist planning are bound to arouse.

It would be foolish not to expect some form of capitalist resistance to socialist planning. Some people will be very unhappy with the proposal to take crucial decisions out of the boardrooms of private (and public) industry, away from Whitehall corridors, and instead ensure that they become social decisions, made openly and with regard to society's needs. Socialist planning would be poorly served by erecting some fancy apparatus that only relocated decisions from private business to the privacy of Downing Street.

The hostility of private interests which do well out of the present set up can surely be overcome. But to do this ordinary people must become convinced that they *can* plan. Trying to persuade people of their ability to make key decisions and to plan is, or should be, a main plank of socialist and Labour Party argument. Instead, as we will see, there is a disturbing hint that the Labour Party and trade union leaders may be coming round to the view that the argument for socialist planning has to be won among employers rather than workers. It is hard to believe that democratic socialist planning can ever be acceptable to existing business interests.

Towards a practical economics for socialists

Chapters four and five look to the future. They examine the most recent planning proposals to have emerged from the TUC and

Labour Party, nationally and in local authorities, and ask, can they work? The main problems are likely to be political rather than technical. It will be no good looking to the 'experts' to build the socialist planning system. The strength in overcoming the political problems standing in the way of socialist planning can only come from the people organised in factories, shops, offices and local communities and equipped with their own vision of an industrial regeneration – one which will benefit them and their families.

The Lucas workers showed the way forward with their alternative plan – a detailed list of socially useful products which they could make while government could help organise sales and purchases. Others followed the same path, as job losses in British industry grew. In motors, machine tools and heavy engineering, workers began to think about developing alternatives to closures threatened by management. To do this they had to reject not just management's conclusions, but the entire profit-maximising logic upon which they were based. Considering those planning initiatives case by case shows workers thinking about social need in a much more meaningful way than any previous Labour government has done. Simultaneously those workers were laying the foundation for a new economics which could challenge the bosses' notions of 'efficiency' and 'competitiveness'. They began to ask, in whose interest is 'efficiency' that demands the sacrifice of thousands of jobs? In whose interest is technological progress that throws people out of work?

It became clear that in developing alternatives to the steps taken by management, workers would have to take control of the process of becoming, as well as defining 'efficient' and 'competitive'. Unfortunately, in the 1970s things did not go as far as they might along this road largely because the Labour government did everything that was possible to prevent workers' plans from becoming a reality. It did this, as we shall see, because it was thoroughly wedded to private capital and the logic of private profits. It had no interest in an economics of social need.

The last chapters show that there is an alternative to the logic of the capitalist market. While that market logic often seems unquestionable, in fact it reflects no more than one particular pattern of decision-making by a few people in pursuit of private profits. It can and should be replaced.

Lucas and other workers have shown how to begin developing

an alternative economics. At this moment some local authorities, notably in London, Sheffield and the West Midlands, are building on that experience. In London for example, there is talk of producing a city-wide plan which would involve Londoners in discussing social and economic needs and how best to use idle resources to satisfy them. It is an uphill struggle, given the deliberate creation of unemployment by the Thatcher government. But those initiatives will prove immensely helpful in winning the argument against waste. At the same time they are making an important contribution to building a genuinely practical economics for socialists – and that is what planning should be all about.

2.

The East European Planning Disaster

Socialists need a practical economics, a guide of some sort to help map out an alternative economic system. The intention is simple enough – to use vast and often technologically sophisticated resources to satisfy social needs. It would be useful if we could call upon some historical experience which might indicate how we should organise to achieve this task. Unfortunately, it is not much good looking at British nationalised industries or the welfare state. Soviet and East European planning is not very helpful either – it is, and always has been, thoroughly undemocratic. But this is far from an argument that socialist planning is bound to end up in the same way. On the contrary, there are strong indications that the direction of any 'inevitability' is the other way round. Soviet planning is likely to have to democratise in order to survive. To see this we need to look more closely at central planning than is customary in British political discussion.

East European planning is inefficient, wasteful and authoritarian. Many East European societies are also extremely unstable. These two features are closely connected. Present economic arrangements promote instability. But it is this instability which may in the end lead to the democratisation of the planning mechanism. Of course it is not a simple matter of one day switching off a worn-out planning machine and switching on another. If East European workers try to grab decision-making power from their thoroughly unrepresentative politburos, then party first secretaries, among others, will of course be rather unhappy. Despite this resistance, everything about East European economic organisation and performance points unmistakably in one direction – to the need for change. To understand this we have to examine what might be called the 'planning dynamic'. We need to understand what makes central planning tick in the peculiarly defective way it does.

How does central planning 'work'?

First steps – an overview of the plan

The basic ideas underpinning the functioning of centrally planned economies are exceedingly simple. Decisions about what should be produced, how the productive apparatus should be utilised and how the result of that activity, the social product, should be distributed between members of society are made in a calculated and deliberate manner by the chief authority in the economic system. In the West those sorts of questions are answered, as it were anonymously, through the market mechanism. That is to say, the contemporary planned economy is distinguished by the existence of a decision-making group that can be identified, and the consequent performance of the economy is largely the result and responsibility of those decision-makers.

This seemingly all-powerful position of the central authority is, however, constrained in a number of ways that become apparent in a more detailed view of the planning procedure. One obvious constraint on the centre is precisely its lack of anonymity. If economic conditions deteriorate there is the ever-present danger that the people will turn on and call to account those well-known decision-makers. Margaret Thatcher and Sir Geoffrey Howe may find some shelter behind slogans such as 'international recession' and 'outside our control', but this was clearly not possible, for example, for Gierek (or, at least, the appeal to world recession to explain the Polish economic disaster was never convincing when the Polish first secretary made use of it in the late 1970s).

The highly centralised decision-making procedures of traditional Soviet-type planning sound implausible. There are millions of individual products in any modern economy and it is clearly impossible for even the highly skilled technical personnel employed in the various state planning commissions to make decisions regarding each and every item. But if the planning boards and politburos cannot embrace detailed discussion of every good produced or to be produced, they can still focus on what are considered to be more important materials and products. If it is impossible to consider every investment decision, it is perfectly possible to scrutinise the social product from the viewpoint of how it should be distributed between overall consumption and overall investment. Further, it is possible to decide how the total of investment funds should be distributed across a small number of broad economic sectors.

The first task in planning is to decide how much investment in total there should be over the coming period. Upon this decision rests the rate of economic growth and the possibilities for satisfying the present consumption demands of the population. The second task faced by planners is to decide on the pattern of that investment and the pattern of current consumption. Investment resources have to be spread across competing programmes and those that win out reveal where the more powerful interest groups in the socialist economy lie. This is because the investment allocation decision is primarily a political one, the outcome of a fierce struggle between various ministers and their supporting staffs. The pattern in the Soviet Union and in Eastern European has been for industry to be favoured over agriculture and services. Within industry, heavy industrial branches – coal, power, iron, steel – are usually favoured as compared to light industry producing consumer goods.

Having paid due regard to broad economic magnitudes – the total social product or output, total investment, total consumption – we come then to the detailed problems of planning. How to ensure the production of the individual nuts and bolts, shoes, vodka, and chocolates upon which investment and consumption both depend?

The plan in detail

The traditional Soviet-type response to the detailed planning task is to assert as much central control as possible over the economic decisions taken in the socialist enterprise. It sounds simple enough, but in fact there are obvious limits to the possibility of gaining full control. One is to do with sheer size. In the late 1960s some reckoned that the Soviet economy produced around 20 million different goods. It would have taken an enormous central apparatus to have handled 20 million production decisions each year. Indeed, there is no way in which planning could manage those decisions without itself becoming a huge and thirsty consumer of scarce national resources. No economy could afford to maintain a planning system which itself constituted a major drain on resources.

It is doubtful that such central planning could even function at all, simply because of the vast demands for information it would necessarily generate! Nor is this a problem whose solution is readily found in larger computing facilities. As we will see, one of the main lessons of the Soviet experience is that there are no purely technical solutions to problems posed in economic planning. The reason is that there is no escaping reliance on *people* at the grass roots for economic information. Because of this the accuracy of that information will always be open to question. In addition, information is unlikely to flow around the system as fast as the central planners like and this undermines central control. Finally, the more detailed the decisions taken by the centre, the more sophisticated co-ordination of those decisions must be. As the co-ordination requirements increase, the need for yet more information and more computing would also increase. A deepening central control over economic affairs would seem to generate ever more demands on the centre's ability to plan.

If central planners wisely do not attempt to consider every product, how then do they proceed in trying to control economic activity? Broad categories of goods must be the starting point since only these can be comfortably handled by the planners. The control of important raw or supply materials gives considerable control over end-products. For example, coal, iron, steel, oil, electricity and cement are the kind of items that will be considered most carefully at the pinnacle of the planning system. The approach adopted is a simple one. For these strategic materials the central planners will draw up a balance sheet for the coming year. On one side of the account, the expected production of the material will be registered. To this will be added existing stocks plus any contribution to supply that can be expected from imports. On the other side, there will be a tally of the uses, including final consumption and exports, to which the material will be put as well as the quantities required by each user. This 'material balance', as it is known to central planners, is the cornerstone of plan construction in the Soviet Union and Eastern Europe.

In the late 1960s, it was reported that the Soviet state planning commission (Gosplan) constructed around 2,000 material balances. Of these, a much smaller number, perhaps 300 or so, might actually be reviewed at senior government level by the council of ministers. When we recall the 20 million different goods produced as the result of Soviet economic activity, it may be appreciated that the central planning that goes on cannot be as all-embracing as is often thought.

Even if the centre recognises that total control over the economy is unobtainable, it has always been considered prudent to aim for maximum possible control. Careful choice of planning instruments and of a planning organisation have been of immense importance in this respect. Plan construction starts from broad political objectives, say rapid growth to be achieved through a fast development of heavy industry. From this point on central planning is organised in a hierarchical fashion. From an overall rate of growth target for the whole economy, the planning board establishes targets for key economic sectors. The economy is organised so that each of these sectors is represented by a branch ministry. Thus we might expect to find a dozen or so ministries ranging from fuel and power, heavy industry, light industry to agriculture. A number of so-called functional ministries will also exist, dealing with foreign trade, labour and wages, or finance. Beneath each of the branch ministries we find productive units – plants, workshops, factories – sometimes amalgamated into larger 'trusts' or 'associations', sometimes simply left as single unit enterprises. As respective ministries receive their preliminary output targets for the next plan period they sub-divide those targets into specific objectives for each subordinate enterprise. Alongside their targets, ministries receive information on input availability which also needs to be broken down and passed down to enterprises as maximum quantities of resources to be expected.

All this happens in the first round of plan construction and it is a period rich in tensions between the various participants. One source of tension is a weakness of the centre which it is always impossible to counteract effectively. That is its lack of complete information on up-to-the-minute economic conditions at plant level. Central planning, as it has unfolded, can be viewed in large part as a game where the centre is only one player constantly trying to use all manner of methods to get the others (the people in the factories) to carry out its wishes. Traditionally, central planning has wanted rapid growth and enterprises working flat out to achieve that objective. In building the plan ambitious targets are passed down, *unaccompanied* by generous input allocations. In this way an element of what is popularly referred to as 'tautness' is built into planning.

Unfortunately for the centre, the enterprises do not want to play this game. They do, however, understand the rules, and the rules dictate that there will be only one exploratory passing down of trial targets and input allocations. In the next round they will receive legally binding targets and resource limits. The first round of the plan building procedure is necessary for the centre to update its economic intelligence; it has to try to find out what production capacities and input demands are likely to arise in the coming year. It needs this information since without it there is no construction of material balances and no central economic planning. The enterprises can also put this first planning round to good use by vociferously arguing against the height of the output targets they have received and by claiming that input allocations are hopelessly inadequate. A sort of 'plan-bargaining' takes place between centre and enterprise. Trying to find an answer to the question – who habitually wins in the bargaining? – is made almost impossible because, of course, both parties realise that they are about to enter a bargaining game long before the first provisional target figures emerge. It is possible that sometimes enterprises end up with relatively 'easy' targets, though given the general economic climate (a permanent dash for growth) and the amount of updating of plans that goes on (in an upward revision of targets) most Soviet and East European firms must generally be faced with awesome economic tasks.

Central planning follows what is known as an 'iterative' procedure. A first set of targets is suggested alongside provisional input availability. These are passed down the planning hierarchy from central planning board via ministry to enterprises. The enterprises relay fresh information to ministries which collate data and pass on to the planning commission the new targets suggested by enterprises and new input requirements. The commission opens its balance sheets for its few thousand key materials and adjusts its initial entries. New targets and input availabilities are settled and relayed to ministries in the final plan document. The ministries in turn distribute targets and resources among their member enterprises. With more 'iterations' – the further upward and downward flow of information and commands – better balanced plans might result.

However, time constrains the planners. The plan for 1983 can be perfectly in balance but it is little use if it only appears in 1984. It is often only well after the year has started that enterprises receive their planned tasks for the current year. A more fundamental problem also appears. In the collation and dispersal of economic data between summit and bottom of the planning pyramid, information is necessarily lost. To put it simply, the centre's 2,000 material balances can be 'perfect' but this still leaves a number of goods which do not enter into balances at the planning commission and are therefore unaccounted for by the centre. Of course, the ministries will look at many more individual items than the state planning commission or the politburo, but it is possible that now and again some goods will be completely overlooked, and, as a result, not produced. In a famous case, hairpins were negligently omitted from one Polish plan and because of this no new hairpins could be found anywhere in Poland in 1957.

Problems in plan implementation

Getting people to behave 'properly'

An enterprise gets its orders from its superior organisation. Why should it execute those tasks? Can the planners ensure that enterprises will toe the central line? Soviet planners have relied on a mixture of carrot and stick with more of one and less of the other depending on broad social and political circumstances. Stalinism was *the* period of the stick. Factory managers in the Soviet Union were often shot or exiled for failure to sustain the tempo of 'socialist' industrialisation. 'Gangsters' and 'traitors', 'saboteurs' and 'spies' were regularly found among workers and suffered the same fate. But even this brutal economic administration was not without its reliance on incentives. Some workers frantically tried to exceed the production norm for the shift in the hope of becoming a 'Hero of the Soviet Union' or a holder of the 'Order of the Red Banner'.

Just how much of a motivating force these moral incentives were can probably never be known given that some of the 'Stakhanovite' workers were less kindly rewarded by their workmates. (The Stakhanovites took their name from a Russian coal miner, Aleksy Grigoriyevich Stakhanov, who was reputed to have dug 102 tons of coal in one shift.) Birkut, the bricklayer hero of Stalinist Poland in

Wajda's film *Man of Marble*, got a red-hot brick for his efforts as he tried to show how much wall could be built with the correct application of mortar plus socialist enthusiasm. Some Stakhanovites were actually murdered by their workmates in the Soviet Union of the 1930s.

The real importance of socialist competition was not that it liberated enthusiasm but that it helped to smash workers' solidarity and so weakened their resistance to the Stalinist regime. Individual rewards, whether financial or moral, divided worker from fellow worker. But just to make sure of the disruption of the working class, the terror was unleashed.

In the post-war period increasing reliance has been placed on financial rewards for good effort but there are problems with this. First of all, there is the difficulty posed by the increased inequality of income in a supposedly socialist society with its strong public and well-advertised attachment to the reduction of inequality. Secondly, there is a problem in gauging the correct 'tension' in the reward system so that money incentives are attractive but neither too easy nor too hard to achieve. Third, people in the enterprise, both workers and managers, sensibly, will attempt to 'plan-bargain' for 'soft' targets. They will certainly not be keen to overfulfil the plan by large margins for fear of setting in motion the unhappy ratchet mechanism that sets next year's targets using current results as a baseline.

More central directives – less central control

It may be permissible for the centre to concern itself with as few as 2,000 key materials but when ministries receive targets and input allocations these figures have to be broken down and translated into numbers that mean something in each enterprise. In the annual plan received by the enterprise from the ministry, there may be as many as 150 formal targets of various sorts. This range typically includes figures for output growth, unit costs reduction, proportion of new products in total output, permissible faulty production, and so on. In fact, there are indicators in the plan to cover every aspect of enterprise operations. Since there are so many indicators some at least are likely to be mutually inconsistent. Paradoxically, the proliferation of these directives gives the management of enterprises a much greater economic freedom than the central planners intend. If all targets cannot simultaneously be achieved, management will focus on the art of the possible.

Among the real possibilities, plant managers will concentrate on achieving the targets that have the highest money bonuses, attached to them. But in addition to the formal directives of the plan, management also finds itself at the mercy of many demands made informally which further complicate the problem of running a socialist enterprise. As if any further complexity were needed, managers find that these tasks often change at short notice.

The socialist firm used to be seen by many as a kind of 'black box' executing faithfully its role in the national economic and social plan. Enough has been said above to indicate the dimensions of the error in considering centrally planned enterprises in this light. By implication it would be mistaken to take a 'technocratic' view of economic planning and the problems it generates.

Central plans and local mafias

Apart from the formal and informal tasks coming from the superior ministry, the East European business manager will have close contact with local authorities and the regional party apparatus. Inside the enterprise, workers have to be kept sweet. As the use of repression disappears (and, despite the Polish setback, the long-run trend is in that direction) it would be a foolish manager who got caught out by an upward plan revision and unco-operative labour force.

As the central plan starts to get executed in the enterprise it invariably becomes clear that the plan has very rough edges. Insufficient or badly structured supplies are a common problem. There may not be enough steel tubing of the correct diameter, or too much of a different variety. Television tube production may be proceeding according to plan but unfortunately the cabinet makers may have found easier ways of fulfilling their particular targets, perhaps by exporting coffee tables to Sweden. Alongside shortages of some critical inputs in certain places stocks of others start to accumulate elsewhere. The railway often does not have the wagons where they are needed and the movement of goods may have more to do with satisfying the ton–kilometre plan than delivering to customers. One lesson is plain – better co-ordination of economic activity is desperately needed.

Once we understand the hierarchical and highly centralised Soviet style of planning it comes as no surprise that East European economies are poorly co-ordinated. Yet in spite of all this the plan somehow does get fulfilled. How can this possibly happen? If enterprise managers, local government officials and low-ranking party people slavishly followed plan instructions, the whole system would most probably seize up under its enormous rigidity. One thing that prevents this is the informal activity for which planned economies are notorious.

Most participants of the planning process are aware of the semi-legal and sometimes illegal activity that must go on if plan targets are to be fulfilled. A factory may not have enough ball bearings to enable it to continue building its lathes but it may have a surplus of steel sheets and skilled workers. The ball bearing factory may be bursting at the seams and have nowhere to store further output. Somehow, a wagon can be arranged if some 'trade' can take place, perhaps some favour done. In certain East European countries it is said that nothing happens before at least a bottle of vodka changes hands. The motto of the fraternity of socialist enterprise managers is, 'you help me with my plan, I'll help you with yours'. The crucial point is that all this happens *outside* the central plan. Technically, it is illegal activity, but without it there would be chaos. So everyone tries to fulfil the plan, at least on paper, using almost any means, and hopes that no one will look too closely. Strong pressures exist which draw managers from different enterprises together with party people in what has been called 'a web of mutual involvement'. This is the local mafia whose main aim is to ensure the fragile planning boat is not violently rocked.

Nothing can be more mistaken than to view Soviet central planning as being managed 'in one grand act of analysis at the highest level'. Plan implementation in the USSR and Eastern Europe has always been an intensely social activity even though its form has been strangely distorted. One distortion occurs in the fact that plans usually only get 'successfully' executed through the illegal actions of many individuals. But there is an even greater distortion than that occurring in plan implementation. This is the way in which plans are built, with the majority of people having absolutely no voice in their construction. The basic source of the waste and inefficiency of Soviet planning lies in this feature – the system's lack of democracy. And because of this, energies that could be utilised in the social interest are left untapped or misdirected to black and grey markets.

Sophisticated techniques – the solution?

It is easy to see why a technocratic view of planning has been so popular at times. Given the anarchy of the market, periodic economic depression, gross income inequalities, and so on, an opportunity to direct economic life centrally seems too good to pass by. However, modern economies are too complex to be driven in this simple way. Apart from that, we are also familiar with the unacceptable face of central planning – its authoritarianism. Socialism has to be understood as a movement for self-emancipation; as a movement that leads people to exercise real power over their lives. They knew this once in the Soviet Union but Stalin had the memory obliterated. In the post-war settlement which gave Eastern Europe to the Soviet Union, central planning was installed throughout the area much as turbines are installed in a power station. Of course, the people were not consulted.

In this atmosphere it was hardly surprising that a school of mathematical economics should flourish in the Soviet Union. It appealed to the leadership through its techniques, its linear programming models and its fashionable 1960s talk of 'optimal planning' purged absolutely of any social content. Always keen to improve the quality of the central plan, at least within the bounds of the existing political system, the Soviet leadership was for a time enamoured of sophisticated planning tools. It was hoped that these might bring the promise of a more perfect, a more complete, central plan perhaps supervised and maintained by a central committee computer.

These ideas have now lost much of their seductive attraction – at least among Western socialists, if not in all the the East European politburos. The so-called 'praxiological' view of planning had little to commend it. This was a particular conception of planning as a pure science concerned with devising rules and information systems to get maximum results for minimum effect. It had exercised an attractive appeal on many minds in earlier years. Maurice Dobb, an influential Cambridge marxist, had subscribed to the view that problems faced in planning were purely administrative. But that was before he witnessed the shooting of Polish workers by the secret police in Poznan in 1956. And that was the time when many people began to question the notion that technical perfection in planning awaited simple administrative innovations.

When the computers finally did appear it became clear that whatever was wrong with central planning could not be put right so easily. With the recent experience of Eastern Europe to hand it would be foolish to imagine that the problems of socialist planning can be readily solved by picking from the catalogue a 'technique' of the most suitable type. The crude material balances we have described are, alone, incapable of keeping the planned economy smoothly ticking over. There is no reason to believe that other devices, though they may be more sophisticated, can by themselves produce better results – only a planning that is popular can do that.

Can central planning survive?

The growth rate slow-down

It may well be that the usefulness of traditional command planning is diminishing with time. Not only are millions of working people becoming increasingly dissatisfied with central planning but even the ruling groups are coming to realise that their planning system is creaking with age. From the viewpoint of those political leaderships the worst fact is that central planning can no longer guarantee fast growth. We were always led to believe that the ability to generate and sustain rapid growth was one of the chief attributes to central planning. For the central planners it is very damaging, both materially and in the wider competition for ideas, to be faced with a growth rate slow-down, and to be forced to reduce plan targets.

Table 1 **Recent annual average percentage growth rates in Eastern Europe and the Soviet Union**

	1976–80 Plan	Actual	1980–85* Plan
Bulgaria	7.7	6.1	4.6–5.4
Czechoslovakia	4.9–5.2	3.7	2.6–3.0
East Germany	4.9–5.4	3.9	5.1–5.4
Hungary	5.4–5.7	3.2	2.7–3.4
Poland	7.0–7.3	1.7	0.0–0.5*
Romania	10.0–11.0	7.2	6.7–7.4
Soviet Union	5.4–5.7*	4.1	3.7–4.0*

* Estimate.
Source: Financial Times, 19 June 1981.

Table 1 shows that not one centrally planned economy met its output growth objective over 1976 to 1980. For the current 1980–85 plan period targets have been set at even more modest levels in all cases except one – the East German. It is true that the recent growth performance of central planning has been better than in most capitalist countries, but this is small comfort to East European leaderships. For them the disturbing feature is that the growth slow-down seems to be a long-run tendency rather than a passing aberration. Furthermore, they are deeply anxious that existing social and political mechanisms in planned economies may be incapable of coping with the strains imposed by deteriorating economic performance. Recent Polish events can only have heightened those anxieties. The evidence is clearly that the combination of central planning plus autocracy is an unstable mix. It is one that cannot come to terms with the problems of managing modern industrial economies.

Social tensions and central planning

East European countries found in the 1960s that growth rates were falling as compared to the 1950s. This was a time when growth as part of the competition to overtake capitalism was still the priority task. The all-important question became – how to sustain growth? An answer was speedily found, which basically made use of that one obvious 'quality' of central planning – the ability to marshal resources and direct them to specific, well-defined uses. Real wage growth could be lowered to free more resources for investment. A slow wage growth would encourage a higher rate of participation by the labour force. More married women would feel the need to go out to work to supplement family income. Some pensioners would also look for work for similar reasons. In this way more labour resources could be found and flagging production growth rates could be accelerated.

In the enthusiasm to use central planning as the solution to the growth rate problem, some political leaderships found themselves forgetting about the people – easily done by party first secretaries. They completely overlooked the problem that workers might not respond well to further rounds of belt-tightening and minimal growth in living standards. Some leaders also overlooked, to their great cost, the fact that the central plan was their exclusive property – a piece of real estate where the people were forbidden to trespass. We have already seen how society had no part in plan construction, despite the rhetoric of people's democracy. When this is put beside the tendency of East European leaders to treat economic problems as purely technical, demanding technical solutions, and their inclination to treat the people as if they are there merely to ensure plan implementation, then problems are likely to arise.

In the end, it was predictable that 'something would give', that working people would only for so long foot the bill for an increasingly expensive economic system. Heavier and heavier doses of inputs were needed to secure modest additional points to the growth rate record. To put it differently, the operation of centrally planned economies was increasingly ineffective. To produce each extra unit of output demanded a disproportionate increase in labour power, machinery and equipment. The social cost in finding those additional resources was invisible to the central authorities and so, in most cases, ignored.

A growing tension has been evident in Eastern Europe between needs (both economic and social) and the inability of the traditional planning system to 'deliver the goods'. It is in this tension that we find the source of East European and Soviet economic discussion since the mid-1950s on the issue of 'economic reform'.

The basic question addressed in that debate has been deceptively straightforward: 'What changes does our central planning need to make it more effective?' For the many East European economists who have studied the problem it has always been tacitly understood that the changes must in no way threaten established privilege. It is because of this constraint that reforms have been so disappointing and this holds even for the most adventurous East European reform, the widely acclaimed 'New Economic Mechanism', introduced in Hungary in 1968.

Political leaders in Eastern Europe are afraid of the long-term consequences of sanctioning any deep reform of central planning. They know that reforms will introduce a new, decentralised pattern of economic decision-making. Where will that leave the traditional decision-makers of the politburo, the central committee, the planning commission and the industrial ministries? The obvious answer is: without much of a future. In the face of such odds the favoured strategy of the authorities seems to be 'better to sit tight and hope for the best' – better to hang on to the old system and hope that somehow economic deterioration can be avoided.

But it is a poor strategy for survival. There is absolutely no reason to expect that the dynamic planning tensions we have discussed will go away. As Maurice Dobb put it in his *Socialist Planning* in 1970,

> it is hardly likely that the new technological age and higher living standards can be contained within the old administrative mould inherited from Stalin's day. Economic problems sometimes acquire a compelling logic of their own. One may well see some rapidly changing alignments and landmarks in the socialist world in the decade that lies ahead.

And how the landscape did change. For a time the most prominent landmark in the socialist world became Gdansk on the Polish Baltic coast. In the meantime, central planning in Poland simply disintegrated.

Planning chaos in Poland

The nose dive of the Polish economy in the 1970s was nothing if not spectacular. Here was a supposedly planned economy careering out of control like a faulty cruise missile. In the late 1970s a former professor of economics at Warsaw University, Wlodzimierz Brus, pointed to the

> paradoxical fact that the economy defended in the name of planning . . . appears increasingly strongly to be drifting under the influence of anarchic processes, controlled neither by market nor by plan.

The main problems are well known: growing inflationary pressure, with more money chasing fewer and fewer goods; a growing trade deficit and greater indebtedness to Western governments and banks; an investment effort grossly overreaching the physical capacity of the economy to sustain it, and meanwhile generating a boost to incomes unmatched by any real output. In short, as economists would put it, massive and chronic 'disequilibrium'.

The basis upon which well-reasoned economic decisions could be made was fast disappearing. Consumers found that access to goods in the shops could be improved only by queuing for long hours. The privileged access to the available output of some in the upper ranks of the party, or in the police, caused understandable resentment. Economic imbalance in consumption was fuelling a wide range of social tensions. In production it was co-ordination of economic processes that first began to show strain. The domestic supply system could not cope with the huge demands being placed on it. The hard cash needed to buy imported supplies was quickly running out.

Polish central planning had disintegrated. It may seem an odd thing to suggest but this was partly the result of an overzealous application of traditional central planning technique. There is a refrain, popular among central planners, that 'if we issue ever more detailed orders we will eventually control all we want in the economy'. Nothing could be more in keeping with central planning tradition – and nothing could be more mistaken. All that the proliferation of directives guarantees is confusion, as the planners overlook both the problems posed by the need for economic co-ordination and the need to win popular support for planning objectives. As economic performance deteriorated the authorities increasingly revealed their inability to control economic events.

The total absence of any opportunity for genuine debate on economic issues was critical in permitting the downward slide to gather momentum. It is hard to believe, but none the less true, that in an economy where the main plank of development strategy rested on borrowing capital from the West, the amount of that indebtedness should remain a state secret until the eventful summer of 1980. The leadership was increasingly content to cocoon itself in an almost make-believe world where the only news permitted to circulate was that which it was pleasing to hear. Nor, it seems, was there any shortage of 'court economists' eager to oblige in the great pretence. There had been an enormous and uncontrolled investment and consumption boom in the early 1970s which should have been seen as a danger signal, but instead became praised as a victory for what the authorities called 'open planning'. In reality this 'open planning' was central planning gone wild. Every above-plan result invited a greater disregard for economic co-ordination and balance. In turn, if imbalance is deep and permanent, social pressures will be generated which can be very difficult to contain. In Poland in the 1970s the road to perdition was paved with above-plan results.

Most people, though cut off from access to real decision-making power, could easily see through the official misinformation on the economic situation. It was likely that eventually even some small event would ignite a massive protest against the social and economic mismanagement of the 1970s. The sparks started to fly when meat prices were increased in June 1980.

The Polish workers take action

A few weeks later, at the end of August 1980, the workers on the Baltic seaboard won the right to organise in independent and self-governing trade unions – *Niepodleglе i Samorzadowy Zwiazki Zawodowe*, to use the Polish. It seems a mouthful. But no one needed a dictionary to understand the significance of *NSZZ–Solidarność*. The Polish workers had taken about all they could and now they acted. Twenty-one demands were put to the authorities who, embarrassed and confused, responded with vacillation and then the characteristic musical chairs among party leaders. But in between the two the workers won. Soon the banners appeared with the victory slogan '21 x *Tak*' (21 x Yes). The leaders of the supposed workers' state were forced to retreat, disorganised and humiliated, in the face of mass protest by the people. Solidarity grew; the party shrank. Among the workers, excited and heated but most of all free, discussions began on the nature of society's accumulated problems. The authorities stood back – for a while.

Of the twenty-one demands, the first two are the best known: the right to organise in free trade unions and the right to strike. They were clearly momentous. The world's press gave them deserved publicity. Much less world attention has been given to the other nineteen demands. And, because of this, we in the West have overlooked the extent to which the Polish workers were making planning as well as industrial demands during their August protest, aimed at the very organisation and running of Poland. They were not simply saying to their government in Warsaw, 'more meat and vodka or we strike', but 'open the books and let's see how *we* can put Poland back on its feet.' In particular there were two demands that related very much to the style of government that workers would approve of in the future.

Demand number three was for freedom of speech and access to the media. In response the authorities promised to draft a new censorship law which would clearly define the type of information that could properly be regarded as secret. The government also promised the media a wider access to socio-economic information. This was absolutely essential if the sixth demand – that the public should be fully informed on economic and social conditions – was to mean anything. The workers demanded that an open debate be launched immediately on the vexed subject of economic reform. The joint statement of the strike committee and government negotiators at Gdansk read:

> Only a nation that is aware of its problems and that has a good awareness of reality can sponsor and implement a programme for streamlining the economy. The Government will radically expand the range of socio-economic information available to the nation, the trade unions and economic and social organisations.

The inter-plant strike committee at the Lenin shipyards was serving notice on the authorities that at least the workers understood that the economic crisis of the late 1970s was largely a result of the lack of honest economic debate throughout society. The Gdansk settlement agreed that each of the following issues would become subject to authentic social discussion:

> the principles of dividing national income into consumption and accumulation [investment]; the distribution of the social consumption fund for various purposes – health, education, culture; the basic principles of remuneration and the lines of wage policy – particularly the principle of an automatic adjustment of wages under conditions of inflation; long term economic plans; investment policy; and changes in prices.

In this way it was hoped that there would be 'genuine opportunities for publicly evaluating the new decisions that determine working people's conditions'. The world's press gave little space to these issues and Margaret Thatcher was uncharacteristically quiet. To this date Downing Street has failed to approve the attempt by Polish workers to take these decisions into their own hands.

It was clear that, if honoured, this agreement was going to have significant implications for Polish central planning. A new type of economic management and control would have had to appear. Of course this was and still is necessary since, even in the absence of the graft, corruption, and simple mistakes of the Gierek years, it was obvious from the long-term performance of both the Polish and neighbouring economies that traditional central planning was worn out. In the short period between August 1980 and the military take over in December 1981, the first steps were taken on the road towards Poland's first socialist plan. Workers began to talk seriously about how they would run the economy to satisfy their needs. Unfortunately for Poland, that road has been blocked by tanks. Military hardware and brute force can silence debate but cannot halt the compelling logic of economic forces about which Dobb spoke. Generals may believe that they are bound to make the best central planners. They are expert at issuing orders and economic commands may seem no different to them – simply militarise key enterprises, put workers under military discipline, tell them what to do, shoot them if they refuse. This is what they may believe and it may appear to work in the short term as society lies in shock. In the end this is not the road to higher productivity or greater efficiency and the satisfaction of social needs. For that Poland will still need the socialist plan that was being developed until December 1981.

Towards a socialist plan for Poland

One of the few commitments of August 1980 which the authorities did honour was to launch a reform discussion. This was a 'safe' and sensible thing for them to do involving as it did much talk and little action. Official reform debates in Poland usually arrive soon after leadership changes have taken place. They are something like the public enquiries or parliamentary select committees of British political life. When a reform commission is set up most Poles yawn and assume the government intends to do nothing. They know that the authorities are really hoping that the relevant problems will go away or be forgotten. Was the discussion of 1980 any different?

There was universal agreement that this reform, like others, had to be about significant economic decentralisation. But where earlier discussions, for example in the 1960s and early 1970s, had focused exclusively on some kind of administrative decentralisation, it now was acknowledged that this was not enough. There was a grave danger, if reform were seen only as an issue to be read along a centralisation–decentralisation axis, that it would develop, as before, an overwhelmingly deadening technocratic character. It would become something for the experts, not for society.

The summer strikes made it clear that reform had to be socially determined. If it was viewed in other ways workers would get nowhere. Decentralisation as a key feature of reform implied a vastly increased role for the socialist enterprise in the planning system. The problem was, how to give this decentralisation its rightful social character? The answer lay in insisting that the crucial reform element must be workers' self-management. This was what distinguished the debate from the 1960s and 1970s discussions. In the new planning system which would be forged by Wajda's 'men of iron' the whole planning process would be from the bottom up.

Not surprisingly the need for workers' self-management was put particularly strongly in the days of August and September 1980. Two Polish journalists summed up this mood at the time in the economic weekly *Zycie Gospodarcze*:

> Workers' self-management is not the destination. Experience, and not only today's, shows that self-management in our society is a point of departure, an absolutely indispensable condition for the progress of economic, social and moral civilization.

Zycie Gospodarcze organised a discussion on self-management in which Solidarity advisers participated. Some of the flavour of the ideas being thrashed out in Poland at the time is given in one journalist's report of that meeting:

> The discussion confirms that we are faced with the enormous problem of socialising the process of economic management, giving it an authentic social character, surmounting any technocratic difficulties which would stand in the way of management by the people. Workers' self-management will be a huge step forward in this respect. It appeared that the nationalisation of the means of production was synonymous with their socialisation and so the whole problem was firmly in hand. It is clear now the problem is definitely *not* in hand. In my view one of the basic sources of conflict was that the process of socialising the means of production was frozen. A bureaucratised, purely formal workers' self-management could not give rise to genuine control. A return to creating a role for workers in economic management creates, despite the damaging economic position, the possibility of solving the most difficult problems of the economy and so too of creating the basis for overcoming social difficulties. We must quickly grasp this opportunity.

That opportunity is now well and truly buried. But had it been allowed to develop, what would central planning in Poland have come to resemble?

There were three notable landmarks pointing in the direction of the new planning. First, workers' councils in workplaces would have provided the lynchpin of economic management. This is where broad, socially agreed plan objectives would have been translated into action. Second, socialist firms would become subject to the three 's's. They would be independent (*samodzielny*), self-managing (*samorzadowy*) and self-financing (*samofinansowy*). This would mean total abandonment of central directives. Government would try to persuade people in enterprises to follow the broad social and economic plan by use of a wide range of tax and financial instruments. Third, the national plan would be agreed in democratic discussion. Solidarity had tried to push in that direction from the very first days in Gdansk. The plan itself would be quite unlike any that had previously been produced. Some had suggested that it should be based on 'social and economic problem areas'. For example, the problem of society's energy requirements or how to improve health, education and housing. The housing shortage in Poland has been, and continues to be, particularly acute. It and other social programmes have always taken low priority compared to the authorities' hankering to expand heavy industry. What was very slowly taking shape in discussion was a planning for social need. The 'social and economic problem areas' would have replaced iron, steel and heavy engineering as the main focus of economic planning.

The authorities were unhelpful in promoting these new directions in economic planning. Their contribution to the reform discussion was disappointing. They focused exclusively on two issues – the hiring and firing of directors, and the election procedures to be followed by workers' councils. There was no feel for wider issues, how workers' councils might fit in with the more general economic reform or the development of future economic policy. They had little to say about central planning. True, they had set up a commission to look into it, chaired by an eminent lawyer. He had spoken commendably but vaguely about the need to 'socialise the central plan' but in the end all that was offered was a wider display of plan variants from which society could choose. The overwhelming failure of the official version of economic reform was its coyness, its reluctance to state clearly where real power lies in the traditional central planning system and how this power should be dispersed. Thus, for example, everyone is aware of the key role played by the party at all levels in economic decision-making, but this was barely hinted at as a problem to be clarified in any new system of economic administration. If the workers wanted to plan it would clearly be without any help from party leaders. An unfortunate but probably inescapable tension was created as Solidarity groped towards a socialist plan for Poland while the authorities were mainly interested in preserving the old system, the source of their power and privileges.

Socialist planning versus central planning

Centrally planned economies have often been kept ticking over only through the use of the most appalling instruments of economic coercion. If asked to choose which is preferable, the discipline of the market or the discipline of brute force and terror, there is little doubt which way most people would turn. In a sense the planning discussion in the West has never moved beyond this point. In our daily lives the media are persuading us that the choice is as simple, stark and plain today as it was in the 1930s. The difficulties of capitalist economies can be excused if the alternative is some kind of 'economics of the Gulag'. The Soviet and East European economies have added immense fuel to this cause by their misappropriation of the label 'socialist'.

The popular view that socialism equals Soviet-type central planning is misconceived. This is not just because of the complete lack of democracy in Soviet economic management, although that is indeed one of the most compelling reasons for rejecting it. It is difficult to see how traditional central planning could function in a developed industrial economy like Britain's, without the whole machinery grinding to a deafening halt. We are back to the compelling logic of Dobb's economic forces which insists that 'central planning is not suitable for the management of modern economies.' Attempts to impose it would almost certainly lead to instability which could be resolved only by the complete overhaul of the planning system.

Sooner or later, this is the 'modernisation' that Eastern Europe and the Soviet Union will have to facilitate. Economic reform debates have so far been half-hearted and most unsatisfactory. The authorities have shown great unwillingness to shift the nature of the economy in any fundamental way. Of course, no one is really surprised by this inactivity. Even in Hungary, which gets most publicity because of its 'market socialism', results have been disappointing. Despite this, the installation there in 1968 of the 'new economic mechanism' (NEM) was an interesting experiment. It was a carefully stage-managed reform. The party kept it under strict supervision. The role of financial incentives was enormously expanded and the new system did have great appeal to those people with skills that could be traded in the market place. But traditional political institutions were still sacrosanct. Real economic decentralisation must be about diluting central power. The defect of the NEM was that economic decentralisation was not to be a vehicle for the dispersal of political power; that had to remain with the party leader, Janos Kadar.

The Polish workers knew what was wrong with NEM. It had been conceived as a purely technical solution to technical problems. When the Hungarian central committee had met in Budapest in 1968, workers' control was not an item on the agenda. In Poland in 1981, a strong workers' control movement developed alongside Solidarity. In July 1981 the representatives of the workers' councils from 150 plants met for their first congress in Gdansk. This movement exercised an important pressure on the general direction of the Polish reform discussion. An understanding seemed to develop in Poland that economic problems were not simply technical and the province of the experts, but social problems demanding popular solutions.

It may still have been unclear in December 1981 how the Polish reform would have worked out in practice, but it was plain that democracy – giving people opportunities for real control over their lives – was its chief element. This made the discussion quite unlike any other in Eastern Europe in the 1970s.

In the Poland of the early 1970s Gierek, the party leader, had chosen the modernisation of industry through Western credits as his technical solution to economic problems. A modern industrial sector would be built and no need to trouble the workers. This alternative to economic reform came unstuck precisely because it was conceived as an *alternative*, rather than as part of a wider package with internal reforms as an essential feature. Traditional central planning cannot cope with the pressures it generates. It needs reform. The only reform that is likely to succeed is one which builds a popular and democratic planning.

The birth of Solidarity brought closer than ever before genuine planning for social need in Eastern Europe. Progress was being made until the movement was, to use the over-polite and misleading expression, 'suspended'. The logic of economic pressures as well as the experience of Solidarity's first eighteen months can neither be indefinitely halted nor obliterated. At some time, sooner rather than later, Polish economic discussion will take up from the point it reached on 12 December 1981.

The overriding characteristic of central planning is its lack of democracy and all else stems from this. The existence of inequality in favour of the privileged life-styles of those who wield power in the present system is not in dispute. It is an affront to socialism that party secretaries and factory managers, army officers and the police have such superior access to material goods in Eastern Europe today. It is worth noting that, at plant level, lack of democracy is one of the most evident similarities between East European socialism and modern capitalism. The worker on the line at Fiat's Turin plant probably has as much say in company policy as the worker on the Togliatti line in the Soviet Union, or the Zeran line outside Warsaw (both, incidentally, funded by Fiat).

The most striking lesson from central planning concerns the meaning of democracy. Eastern Europe shows again and again the need for the motto of the genuinely socialist planning commission to be, 'against waste and inequality: for democracy'. Now and again, Eastern Europe's leaders are jolted into acting against waste and inefficiency. On occasion the knock is hard enough for democracy to become a respectable topic of conversation. Sometimes, the groundswell for democracy actually knocks first secretaries off their pedestals. Often a mere change in personnel is enough to disarm protest. But people learn from past mistakes and sooner or later the demand for democracy in Eastern Europe is going to be irresistible. Then, as the East German dissident Rudolph Bahro put it, 'the locomotive of history will move on to the next station.'

3.

Planning in Britain

Britain, like many other developed capitalist countries, has had its own experience of economic planning. At times planning has been enthusiastically courted; at other times it has been described as the greatest impediment to the further growth of the nation's economic strength or even as a threat to civilisation. Some may be surprised, given the currently well-advertised 'virtues' of market forces, that there was ever a time when planning was respectable. Yet British governments *have*, on several occasions, suspended, or greatly modified, the operation of the market. These have been times when the economic tasks facing the country have been daunting and the market mechanism simply unreliable. In those circumstances the authorities have decided that it was best to take charge of matters directly and *ensure* that the economy moved in the required direction, not that which may have resulted from traditional capitalist decision-making.

The best known examples of British planning occurred during the two world wars. Of course this is not to suggest that what we saw then in any way resembled socialist planning. But, as technical exercises, the national planning that existed then worked extremely well, and because of this it invites inspection. In the post-war period a number of British governments have tried to plan – without much enthusiasm and with even less success. Since they were predominantly Labour governments engaged in planning, and since planning is again on the Labour Party agenda we must ask what went wrong. There may be some valuable lessons tucked away in this planning experience. We might find something that can contribute to developing a practical economics for socialists.

The British economy at war

No war can be fought unless armies are raised and equipped. For any economy the basic problem in the transition from a peace to a war footing is how to develop and nurture an armaments industry as rapidly as possible. Why not let the market solve the problem? The government could simply announce its new demands; ask for tenders for guns, bayonets and uniform buttons, and leave the rest to market forces. But from a theoretical viewpoint trouble can be foreseen. Greater demand leads to higher prices – not just for military hardware but also for the materials required for its production. The authorities might well find the final bill presented to them to be substantially higher than they want to pay. Meanwhile, higher prices for goods elsewhere in the economy, but particularly for consumer goods, would make life very difficult for poorer members of society.

If the authorities were to insist on 'planning through the market' in this way, higher prices would be inevitable. This would be the only way of indirectly influencing capitalists' decisions and encouraging private business to tilt industry in the desired military direction. Higher prices would lead to higher profits which would signal to 'entrepreneurs' that rich pickings are to be found in arms production. Private decision-making would channel capital and labour resources to munitions and other warlike activities. Other sectors of the economy would shrink, unless the capitalist economy had been one suffering from unemployment before the hostilities started. In that case the waste of unemployment gets translated into production of the most wasteful goods that can be imagined – armaments. But the economic problems of war are not only high prices, unpatriotic profit-taking, or shortages. Time is of the utmost importance. The market might deliver the 'goods' to the generals but how long does it take? What if private producers respond too slowly? What if in some cases they choose not to respond at all? Who for example would want to invest in a munitions factory in the age of aerial warfare? These factors considered, it might be better to substitute the decisions of central government for the decisions of individual capitalists. It might be preferable for the government to plan.

The most persistent problem of organising a war economy is that something known as an 'inflationary gap' is unavoidably created. It has its source in the structural changes taking place. Incomes are generated in the production of tanks as much as in the production of family cars but, as car output diminishes and tank output grows, there is much less to spend that income on. Real wages fall with an absolutely smaller supply of consumer goods. Those with higher incomes are cushioned, to the extent that they can afford the higher prices that will be charged. Others have to accept that 'the market' has nothing for them. People without purchasing power are simply pushed out. Higher market prices ration the available supply among the people but only in a grossly unfair way.

Any government that permitted the market to 'solve' the problem of the inflationary gap in this way through higher prices would deserve to lose the war. And it most probably would lose. If the sacrifices imposed by war were not seen to be reasonably equally shared among people, resentment would grow, morale suffer and, and in all likelihood, fighting spirit would evaporate. There is obviously a strong need to intervene in the marketplace to ensure an equitable access to limited consumption possibilities. It is ironic that in wartime, capitalist economies become much more vigorously concerned with equity than in peacetime.

Price and wage controls and rationing are as important to the prosecution of war as are armies at the front. The domestic economy becomes subject to ever more detailed controls as the planning apparatus extends itself to meet the tasks demanded of it. But there is a limit both to the possibility of controlling economic transactions and to the need for their control. We have seen how the Soviet planner often ends up controlling less by issuing more detailed economic commands.

How the war economies were planned

At the start of war in 1914 no planning blueprint lay hidden away in some war ministry filing cabinet. Planning skills had to be acquired through the hard school of experience. The same was true at the outbreak of the second world war. Planning developed in an ad hoc manner. The government acted in the economy, the market responded and the response was found wanting. The government compensated for the inadequate market performance by judiciously extending controls until the market was subordinated to the single aim of fighting war.

A particularly clear example of the development of British wartime planning and of the manner in which controls grew and extended themselves is given by sack production during the first world war. Sacks served a variety of military purposes ranging from horse nosebags to trench construction. As the war progressed it became plain that the army's demand for sacks was prodigious and growing due to the military stalemate on the Western front. The economic historians of the war, W. K. Hancock and M. M. Gowing, explained in *The British War Economy*:

> Towards the end of 1914 the infantry were beginning to dig as infantry had never dug before. They kept on digging throughout the war . . . Towards the close of 1914, the army was calling for bags at the rate of about a quarter of a million a month. By May 1915, it was demanding six million a month.

The war ministry went into the market for sacks but met with a noticeably weak response from producers. Whether there was a real shortage or some incipient speculation was not at first clear. The authorities issued an urgent appeal for sacks in early 1915 but still the response was poor and they

> received a swarm of unsatisfactory small offers, together with one large offer from a speculator who hoped to corner the whole supply of sacks and make a 100 per cent profit by selling them to the government at a price three times higher than the previous market price.

The authorities were stung into action by this 'impudent proposal'. They went to Liverpool and requisitioned the stocks of sacks held by merchants and quickly followed this up by direct action against the sack producers located mainly in Dundee. The army's demand was given priority and the producers simply had to break any earlier private contracts they had entered into.

A problem arose in deciding on the appropriate price for sacks. The Liverpool merchants were paid the price that had ruled before the war ministry entered the market. Justice demanded a similar treatment for the manufacturers. In the end they got a price reflecting the authorities' view of costs plus a 'fair' return. In this way economic control began to extend itself deeper throughout the industry in a vertical penetration from merchant to producer. Soon the government found that this was not a straightforward matter since many firms in the industry dealt only with particular stages of the manufacturing process. The authorities found that, whether they liked it or not, control meant becoming involved in ever greater detail with each firm in the industry. Prices and 'just' profit rates had to be set not only for the final product but for each stage of the manufacture. A daunting task, perhaps – but one that was achieved.

What emerged as a result of this extension of control was a system of planning that relied on greatly modified and constrained market mechanisms to bring about the desired production results. Centrally determined prices and rates of return encouraged producers themselves to make the decisions of which the government would approve. The delicate 'pulls' of the market remained intact as a planning instrument but, at the same time, controls in one sector of the economy soon highlighted the need for controls in other sectors in a horizontal penetration of planning. Sack production, for example, required jute as an input. Steps taken to boost sack output would probably lead to difficulties in other industries also dependent on jute like, say, linoleum. The authorities would have to devise some suitable rationing of the raw material among various producers. And, of course, they did this successfully.

An ever larger and more complex planning apparatus had to be set up and maintained. Departments responsible for particular goods and inputs soon emerged. Alongside the growth of planning there also grew the danger of economic chaos, should co-ordination of economic processes not be mastered. As Hancock and Gowing put it:

> it became apparent that the unchecked competition of departmental administrators would cost the nation no less dear than the unchecked competition of individualist buyers and sellers.

Some well-defined overriding authority was required at the peak of the planning apparatus both to oversee the general progress of planning and to adjudicate between competing claims on critical resources. A committee of the war cabinet was set up with this purpose in mind. Once again it seems to have been generally successful in mediating conflicting demands, particularly, during the first world war, the claims made on shipping by various departments.

In the second world war, after a slow start, an elaborate system of economic controls was erected. But alongside these controls price and profit signals were allowed to act as incentives, attracting producers and labour into war industry and away from other sectors. In this way the market was allowed to exercise its 'pull' on the economy. The 'pushes' provided by government were, however, pretty extensive. These consisted of: controls over the use to which premises could be put, requiring a permit when a change of activity was desired by any producer over a certain size; controls over inputs, requiring licences to be obtained before access to materials and machinery was granted; powers enabling labour conscription; and, finally, in exchange for the extensive controls obtained, the authorities had to strike a bargain with labour over wages, prices and access to goods in a kind of 'national economic assessment'. The consent of working people for the operation of the new economic regime was purchased with price control, excess profits tax, and the rationing of essentials.

One of the most impressive results of wartime planning was its success in mobilising resources and getting them smoothly into priority areas of economic acticity. At first the process was slow. For example, it is hard to believe that some eight months after the outbreak of war over one million people in Britain were still unemployed. However, the catastrophic defeat at Dunkirk in May 1940 saw to it that a new and total commitment would be given to the war effort. By June only 645,000 were still out of work. As the war continued the unemployment total was further reduced until, by the time of the Normandy landings in 1944, it stood at only 54,000.

An interesting casualty in the transition to total war over 1939–40 was something that had been known in earlier years as 'the Treasury view'. This was essentially a statement relating to what the nation could or could not afford. The Treasury guarded the books and made sure that the national housekeeping was conducted firmly in the black. Throughout the economic blight of the 1920s and 1930s, the orthodoxy was that the nation's financial affairs had to be attended to with the same prudence that applied to the corner shop. In the end the cost of adhering to this conventional wisdom was to condemn millions of British workers to long years of unemployment. The books might balance or even show a surplus but meanwhile real resources, labour and machinery, lay idle.

It became clear after Dunkirk that this economics of the madhouse could not be afforded in wartime. With its rejection went also the 'eclipse of the Treasury' as Paul Addison puts it in his book, *The Road to 1945*. He also explains that an important economic lesson learned was that 'in total war it was essential to plan resources first, leaving the financial side to be adjusted accordingly'. As a result, the authorities began to look at the economy in new ways. Manpower and other real resource budgets, similar to the material balances of Soviet planning, proved much more useful than the money income and expenditure statements of traditional accounts. These resource budgets and the simple arithmetic they contained were the stuff of wartime planning.

Many more things became possible when the Treasury was no longer in a position to impose its criteria of what the nation could afford. In the summer of 1940 a whole range of new welfare schemes was introduced, including free or subsidised milk for nursing mothers and the under-fives, as well as free school meals. Yet only a few months before, in August 1939, the Treasury had declared these schemes to be 'financially impractical'. It takes a second or two to appreciate the rich irony of the situation. When unemployment was well over one million with all the lost output that meant, the Treasury could not 'afford' extra social services; such welfare measures were 'financially unsound', the resources were 'not available'. The Treasury view was blind to the waste stemming from unemployment. Of course it was perfectly possible to have good provision of social services all along; it was simply a matter of prorities. Welfare schemes were important in wartime and so they *were* provided.

The fact that Treasury criteria were overruled in deciding on what was possible, plus the development of a wide range of welfare services, in no way implies that wartime planning was socialist planning. At the outbreak of war the market system had to be prompted to move speedily, and with harmful side-effects minimised, to a new pattern of activity with war production at its focus. Nothing in any of this challenged the private enterprise system. Indeed, to watch over it and to ensure that the fragile mechanism was undamaged in the shift to war, many business people found themselves occupying key roles in the emerging planning apparatus. Thus, for example, a dozen senior Unilever employees occupied important positions at the ministry of food. The match controller actually worked for Bryant and May and had his office on their premises. The paper controller was the chairperson of Reed paper merchants, and so on.

In the end, economic pulls and pushes of various sorts came together and produced an efficient war economy, that is, one that permitted war to be vigorously fought. The reach of the controls was great, much greater than anything that had been known in peacetime. The Board of Trade's involvement in clothing for example even went as far as stating the number of buttons, pockets and pleats which could be officially tolerated. It introduced the nation to trousers without turn-ups as a material-saving measure. The wide panoply of controls was not, as many expected it to be, clumsily bureaucractic. The administrators of the war economy produced results which, all things considered, won wide approval.

In the British economy at war, the authorities were also aware of the limitations of economic control. Take for example the markets in second-hand goods and for luxuries which it would have been foolish to try to control. Nor was any attempt made. The existence of these unregulated markets was in any case useful because they soaked up some of the excess purchasing power running through the economy. It was a matter of good judgement to decide precisely where controls should stop. This judgement seems to have been successfully exercised in the UK war economy.

Lessons for socialist planning

The market system of economic organisation with its private decision-making is by no means the best system of organisation for all economies at all times. The market mechanism was successfully disciplined and constrained to act as the mere instrument of the wartime planner. Indeed, had the economic tasks posed by war been left to market forces it is doubtful that they would have been accomplished. What are the lessons in this experience for socialists?

First, economic planning is certainly feasible. As a planning framework emerged so of course did new economic problems, most of which were satisfactorily solved. It is often argued that because no blueprint for socialist planning in the 1980s exists, the planned 'alternative' must be inadequate. But the experience of economic administration in wartime clearly shows that society has a vast capability to cope with emerging difficulties. While there is no reason to believe that socialist planning will solve all problems as soon as it is applied, there is every reason to believe that solutions can be found to whatever problems arise. All the more so when, unlike the destructive aim of the war economy, a socialist system will be identified by its dedication to promoting social welfare and raising living standards. It is hard to believe that the latter will not generate a much greater fund of commitment and enthusiasm than the former.

Second, there is no reason why planning should not make use of the market mechanism. This may sound illogical but all that it means is that economic decision-making should be, as far as possible, decentralised. During the war, capitalist businesses were left to make decisions under the strong influence of government. In a system of socialist planning workers in the firm should decide on the future direction of its activity. There would need to be some 'rules of the planning game' such as an insistence that firms be self-financing or else that loss-making enterprises subject themselves to a properly organised social audit on the basis of which society as a whole could decide on the firm's future. The important point is that a system of socially concerned, open decision-making would replace the profit-oriented private decison-making of the capitalist enterprise.

Third, we saw that consent was a prerequisite for successfully running a war economy. The greatest problem of war economies is political rather than narrowly economic. Without society's consent the economic measures taken are likely to be ineffective. There are huge differences between wartime economic planning and socialist planning but a socialist economy cannot be built unless it too has the support of the people. The Soviet experience shows that the imposition of a planning system on an unwilling population, while it may produce electrification, falls a long way short of socialism.

The first post-war Labour government

The war experience settled any earlier doubts regarding the appropriate role of the state in a modern economy. The controlled war economy had been seen to function well in adverse circumstances. The 'principles' of economic wisdom guarded by the Treasury had been exposed in all their emptiness. At last, in the new common sense, unemployment was seen to be simply wasteful and therefore would no longer be tolerated. One of the most fundamental changes brought by the war was that governments accepted it as their responsibility to take action to avoid mass unemployment – or so it seemed for a time. Government devised instruments which would shape total spending in the economy. The only kind of unemployment that post-war capitalism would tolerate was the so-called 'frictional' unemployment of voluntary job-switching.

The wartime enthusiasm for planning was extended to peacetime by the Labour government of 1945. Most people believed it right that the state should take over and run certain key industries. There was a general hope that economic and other social decisions would at last be made with an eye to society's needs. Workers looked forward to a new age of security and participation in running nationalised industries. Socialism was not only a respectable subject of conversation; it was on the political agenda. The curtain was raised on the welfare state. No one would have to worry about doctors' bills or a decent education for their children; health, education and housing would be provided by the state. It would also provide a social security system as a safety net to eliminate poverty in post-war society.

The job creation presided over by that first Labour government has much contemporary relevance. Of course, there was no huge army of the unemployed seeking work in 1945 but there were huge armies of servicemen and women eagerly awaiting the return to civilian jobs. This demand for employment was met by the creation of around one million jobs each year from 1945 to 1948. The greatest expansion (709,000) was, as might be expected, in construction. This was followed by services (656,000) then by manufacturing (491,000) and distribution (433,000). Of course, many women who had been drawn into production during the war lost their jobs as munitions production was run down. Finding jobs for them was no part of the post-war programme. None the less our history seems to show us that not only can we successfully plan economic affairs in war but jobs can be generated as quickly as they are needed in peacetime.

An interesting feature in this pattern of job creation is that jobs were obviously opened up in areas where society's need was greatest following wartime privations – construction and services. But, in addition, these are labour-intensive sectors, just the kind that should be focused on when millions of new jobs must be speedily created. Construction and services are also economic branches which are probably least dependent on imports and this is a factor of some significance to the UK economy of the 1980s. Expansion of these sectors could probably take place without much of a strain being placed on the balance of payments.

A post-war boom in economic activity was to be expected. Spending power had been accumulating during the war when consumption had been squeezed to provide military output. Now the economy could shift gear again. The war economy could be run down; resources could be moved into satisfying the needs of the people. The authorities found that, though they had a planning apparatus, this kind of economic shift could take care of itself. People wanted to spend, industrialists wanted to take advantage of growing consumer demands. Inflation was not considered to be a particularly serious problem and nor was the speed with which consumption demands were satisfied. Simple market interactions began to shape economic development much more than central government's planning machine.

A kind of peacetime planning *was* inaugurated by the Labour government of 1945 with its so-called 'annual economic surveys'. These looked to the year ahead and explained in some detail how government saw the economy developing and how resources would be used. But no real attempt was made to shape that development and, in any case, things seemed to be going reasonably well. By 1952 the economic survey had been turned into a review of the past year's economic performance. Neither the theory nor the practice of planning was advanced by Attlee's government. True, it did lay the basis of what is sometimes decribed as a new 'collectivism' where the state spends to maintain full employment, has nationalised industries and supports a welfare state. But even the Tories, in their long reign from 1951 to 1964, could keep all of this without offending their private business supporters. There was however one major exception to this otherwise nice consensus – the nationalisation of steel. And therein lies a tale of much relevance to later attempts by Labour governments to build plans and industrial policies.

The limits to nationalisation – steel

Why should steel prove so troublesome at a time when many other nationalisations caused hardly the bat of an eyelid? The main feature of the early post-war nationalisations was that they were all in sectors where huge losses were being made. The nationalisations were straightforward because private enterprise no longer wished to shoulder the burdens involved. Steel was different. The owners still found themselves managing profitable enterprises. In addition, many felt that should Labour succeed in nationalising steel a dangerous precedent would be set. The existence of good profits might have been reason enough for this view, but there was another point. Steel was not so well or narrowly defined an industrial sector as say, coal or railway transport. Many steel producers also engaged in a variety of manufacturing activities. As Doug McEachern has put it, in the journal *Capital and Class*:

> The finishing sections, and those which concentrated on the production of specialised steels, were almost indistinguishable from other manufacturing industries which used basic steel as their raw material . . . For the first time Labour attempted to nationalise an industry which was not unambiguously infra-structural.

Public ownership of steel would at the same time bring the state dangerously close to possessing its own stake in manufacturing. Private industry feared that an appetite for further nationalisation might be whetted. What is more, Labour governments might develop a taste for profitable industry and not necessarily feel limited to those sectors like coal, gas and electricity which provided essential supplies to private manufacturers. Business opposition to steel nationalisation was fierce because the state had to be kept away from profitable manufacturing industry. Where otherwise would the process of nationalisation end?

The Labour Party tries again – the road to the national plan

Under a succession of Tory governments in the 1950s the detailed industrial planning of wartime was allowed to fade completely away. The 1950s were the years when Keynesian demand management reached its zenith. One way or another unemployment was kept down to under 2 per cent of the labour force. In the 1980s it seems unbelievable that a Conservative Chancellor could ever have appeared on television announcing precautionary steps to expand the economy because of a fear that unemployment might be about to grow. Yet Heathcote Amory did just that in 1961. Detailed microeconomic intervention (actually getting involved in individual markets) was the last thing on anybody's mind when it seemed that unemployment could be kept down simply by regulating spending in the economy as a whole. An attractive feature, to business, of the instruments used by the authorities to adjust spending was their indirect nature. The government could achieve its economic objectives without coming too close to individual markets. Whether in fact the economic performance of the 1950s was due to skilful demand management or to other measures is still a matter of debate among economists. The other possibility was that government economic policies were simply decoration on an economic cake growing bigger because of a boom in international trade. Whatever the reason the Tories showed no interest in microeconomic planning.

In the opposition Labour Party of the 1950s the structure of socialism, as it had previously been perceived, was being redesigned. Anthony Crosland was the architect of the new socialist house. One of its main foundations was the view that the nature of capitalism had changed fundamentally in the post-war period. Crosland argued that ownership of the means of production was becoming an irrelevant consideration in industrial society. The divorce between ownership and control of large enterprises meant that nationalisation had lost its point. The concern of a socialist government should be with economic growth and it should tailor its policy to suit that new objective. To encourage productivity growth, some kind of economic planning would be required. That planning would be characterised by great expertise. Workers' control, or the extension of democracy by some similar device, was rendered unnecessary by the already changed structure of the British economy. We were being prepared for the time when future Labour governments would expertly run the economy of behalf of us all and with no need for us to worry about the details.

A glance at Europe in the 1950s showed economies growing much more quickly than in Britain. Unemployment may never have gone beyond 2 per cent, but in the growth league Britain was a laggard. Some European countries appeared also to implement economic policies that were not used in Britain. Indeed while a simple commitment to the management of overall demand was the main feature of British economic policy, some other countries seemed to be much more active planners.

French planning commanded particular attention. The Keynesian National Institute of Economic and Social Research in London was one of the first British organisations to express real interest in the French experience. That interest was great enough to support a conference at the Institute in 1961 which starred the best-known planner in Western Europe, the French planning chief Pierre Massé. It soon became clear that the aim of French planning had been to reduce uncertainty and to encourage business to invest. The authorities would, in consultation with private business and *sometimes* with the trade unions, fix a desired rate of economic growth for the years to come. The idea was that by indicating its preferred growth rate, private enterprise would see what the government wanted and it would go along with that 'indicative plan', especially in investment decisions. The desired growth rate would then become a self-fulfilling prophecy.

The Labour Party, while still in opposition in the early 1960s, found the appeal of indicative planning irresistible. It was, fortunately, a planning system which could easily be distinguished from Stalinist planning and which already existed in at least one capitalist economy. With indicative planning – a planning of compromise, with targets mutually agreed between government, trade unions and business – the Labour Party felt it had acquired the missing instrument with which to guarantee British economic success. Crosland hoped Labour would appeal to the electorate as the party that really understood how the capitalist economy had changed over time, now that it alone had found how to translate that theory into the practice of indicative planning. With this theoretical and practical package for running a modern capitalist economy, this claim seemed unshakeable.

Planning by the 'white heat of technological revolution'

Labour promised to preside over the technological revolution necessary to modernise British industry. It showed that it had the equipment to manage the 'white heat' generated. The reward was election to government in 1964. Soon the economic planning started in earnest. A five-year national plan was drawn up. The Labour leadership, being distrustful of the Treasury where almost all government economic expertise was concentrated, set up a planning ministry known as the Department of Economic Affairs. The planning minister was George Brown.

The 'indicative' annual economic growth target was set at 4 per cent. It was a surprise to find the national plan assumed that imports would grow at the same rate as output, but exports would grow by 5.25 per cent per annum. This was a surprise because nowhere else in the plan was it suggested how this vast improvement in the competitiveness of British exports was to be achieved. About this and other matters there was a certain amount of vagueness. This was not altogether unusual in indicative planning, targets relying as they do on persuasion as the chief planning instrument. The theory was that once enough people became convinced by government targets, they would act as if those targets were actual outcomes and by so doing they would ensure their realisation. In the British case no amount of pure conviction was – or could be – enough to improve competitiveness. Detailed policies would have had to be elaborated. The plan did not do this. Labour's election manifesto also revealed an unwillingness to talk in any detailed way about planning instruments. It said simply:

> within the national plan each industry will know what is expected of it, and what help it can expect – in terms of exports, investment, production and employment . . . If production falls short of the plan in key sections of industry . . . then it is up to the government and the industry to take whatever measure is required.

As economic events unfolded, it became clear that, sure enough, import growth was considerably faster than export growth. Short-term balance of payments problems soon commanded all attention. A kind of crisis management imposed by the trade deficit took precedence over the long-term growth objectives of the plan. The national plan finally lost any significance when the government slammed on the economic brakes to reduce imports. The Department of Economic Affairs was slowly run down and finally closed in 1969. The Labour Party had failed to restore the competitiveness of British industry through its supposedly deep understanding of recent changes in the capitalist economy. What white heat there was about had vaporised the national plan. The Labour Party, having failed the test of practice, went on to lose the general election of 1970.

Scaling the 'commanding heights' with Labour in the 1970s

From 1970 to 1973 Edward Heath tried to introduce the economics of the 'free market' unspoilt by any widespread state intervention.

Market forces ruled – until the collapse of Upper Clyde Shipbuilders and Rolls Royce. The government responded by making its celebrated U-turn. Legislation was introduced through the Industry Act of 1972 permitting deep state involvement in industrial affairs. Cash was dispensed to preserve jobs and Heath's comprehensive re-education in economic matters was completed. It all took less than two years.

In the meantime, a very important economic discussion was going on in the Labour Party, at least in high-level party committees. It was led by Stuart Holland and its conclusion equipped the Labour Party with a new theory of state economic intervention and new instruments of economic policy. These were the National Enterprise Board (NEB) and system of 'planning agreements' which between them certainly caused a stir in business circles in the 1970s.

The Labour Party found its new planning scheme by following three landmarks. The first was the well-signposted slow growth of the British economy. The second was to note certain weaknesses of the traditional post-war demand management techniques for running modern capitalist economies. The third was to observe in some healthier European economies instruments of economic policy which were unknown in Britain. The result was to suggest that the state could overcome the lack of competitiveness of British manufacturers by itself acting as an entrepreneur. This would mean that traditional beliefs about the purpose of public enterprise, based on the experience of past nationalisations, would have to be revised.

Britain was an economy trapped in a vicious circle of low investment and low growth. Bids to escape from this unfortunate pattern had come to nothing. Meanwhile, many European capitalist countries enjoyed the fruits of a virtuous circle of economic events with high investment fuelling high growth, providing resources for *both* investment *and* consumption, leading to further growth, and so on.

A critique of Keynesianism was the second key element in the argument for the NEB. It was alleged that there were two major difficulties which orthodox post-war economic policy had not come to terms with. The first was the inability of demand management to solve certain economic problems of a 'structural' type, such as securing not just investment but the right type of investment, or ensuring balanced growth across different parts of the country. Second, it was argued that these difficulties were in turn rooted in institutional and structural features of modern capitalism, such as the growth of monopoly, the acceleration in industrial concentration and the rise in power of multinational enterprises.

So it was argued that the economy needed a demand stimulus to put it on a high growth rate cycle. This would provide an incentive for greater investment, plus some means of intervention on the supply side of the economy which would compel the 'right' sort of investment. The former presented no difficulties beyond the capability of traditional Keynesian tools, but clearly new instruments would be needed for the latter task. Outright socialisation of all the largest firms in the economy was rejected by the Labour Party in favour of what seemed to be a much more subtle device. To understand it properly we have to turn for a moment to economic theory.

Economists refer to markets dominated by a small number of large firms as 'oligopolistic'. The emergence of oligopoly has rendered much of conventional orthodox economic analysis obsolete, even in its own terms, though in the textbooks, by sleight of hand and misallocation of space, we are encouraged to overlook this. The feature of oligopoly that makes its analysis so troublesome for most economists is that, given so few firms in any market, it is quite obvious that the decisions of one will have serious repercussions for other firms sharing the market. There is, in other words, very strong interdependence between firms. There is also great uncertainty. No one firm is sure how others are going to behave in the near future.

There may be a clearly identifiable leader in the oligopoly pack. When it makes some movement others may be expected to follow suit. Indeed there is much evidence in oligopolistic markets that prices do move in parallel and that there is often little genuine price competition. If it occurs, rivalry between firms takes the form of new marketing schemes, product development, or investment in cheaper processes. As one firm acts in any of those areas, others will watch closely and aim to respond as effectively as possible. The subtlety of Holland's case for new public ownership was that the state, by investing in a holding company with an economy-wide spread, would in effect become an oligopolist. Since the state is financially extremely powerful it could ensure that it became a leading, rather than a led oligopolist. With the strongest firm from each important industrial sector in its grasp the state could dictate to each one the broad policy it should follow. The commands could be as detailed as 'invest in South Shields', 'invest in microprocessors', 'reduce export prices', or whatever. Once a few leading manufacturing firms embarked on an economic programme, orchestrated by the state, oligopoly would do the rest in correcting the structural problems of the economy. The argument is that other firms because of their interdependence and their 'respect' for the oligopolistic leader (or rather the discipline it could impose) would follow its decisions. For the Labour Party the beauty of the argument, which should also have served to widen its appeal, was that complete state ownership of industry was no longer necessary to build an economy satisfying socialist objectives.

In opposition the argument was elegantly developed. The next Labour government should set up a state holding company – the National Enterprise Board. The state should purchase outright a number of companies in key industrial sectors. These should be the dominant firms in each branch. In total, the NEB should own 25 of the top 100 British manufacturing firms. With such a weighty portfolio, decisions implemented by those firms would, it was hoped, be enough to encourage and shape desirable behaviour in other large British companies. However, just to make certain, the NEB would be set in a broad economic planning framework where other firms would also be drawn in a web of planning agreements with government and unions. Around a hundred planning agreements would be concluded. In return for government grants and subsidies, firms would be expected to say how they would shape their policy to fit in with government's economic intentions. This was the powerful planning apparatus with which Labour would stake its renewed claim to manage the economy and to solve those irksome structural difficulties mentioned earlier. A new surge of life would be given to the British economy by the state acting as a purposeful and caring entrepreneur.

Finally, to add the European dimension, Italian experience seemed to give encouragement to the development of Labour's new 'socialist challenge'. Italy had enjoyed rapid growth over the 1950s and 1960s. It had also had to cope with a notoriously difficult regional problem. The south of the country was predominantly a peasant economy. There was little industry and living standards were poor. The contrast with the industrial and well-developed north was sharp. Despite this, in one or two places, it seemed that some inroads were being made in tackling the regional problem. What was responsible for this rapid national growth and at least the suggestion of a solution to the regional problem?

High investment was certainly a feature of some importance. In addition, and perhaps contributing to that investment, was state enterprise. This was not merely a set of nationalised industries of the British type. In Italy the state held shares in many large manufacturing concerns. Indeed, some it owned outright. All these shareholdings were managed by a state holding company, the Institute for Industrial Reconstruction, or as it is known in Italy, 'IRI'. Here was a novel instrument of economic policy which could complement on the supply side the focus on demand of post-war Keynesianism. NEB was to be the English translation of the Italian IRI.

To summarise the basic argument: demand management, or the state's control of spending in the economy, provided an economic 'pull' which desperately needed to have some 'push' associated with it. According to Stuart Holland this would be provided by the 'harnessing of the oligopolistic follow-my-leader effect' through the new instruments of NEB and planning agreements.

So much for the theory; what about the practice? What happened to Labour's elegant new planning system when, in 1974, the people turned their backs on the muddle produced by Heath's shifting economic philosophy? The time was right for a well-considered state intervention in the economy. Labour seemed to have the goods, but could it deliver?

Planning in practice – the state entrepreneur goes bust

The props of Labour's planning system were put on public display in the mid-1970s. The 1975 Industry Act signalled the birth of both a National Enterprise Board and of planning agreements. However, it soon became evident that the planning apparatus lacked substance. Shortage of real content was conveniently disguised at the time by a spurious air of feverish activity. Labour ministers were eager to show the speedy results of their intervention in the economy. A taste of this unstinting enthusiasm was given by an exchange in the House of Commons in 1976, when Jeff Rooker asked whether 'the Secretary of State is satisfied with the way the NEB is discharging its employment responsibilities?' An industry minister, Les Huckfield, replied, 'Its subsidiaries already employ more than a quarter of a million people in the UK.' It certainly seemed like action on a grand scale. Government ministers would hardly brag about the NEB or exhibit its size as evidence of the transformation to which they were subjecting British capitalism unless they could be sure of supporting their case. Or would they?

What had happened in real terms between 1975 and 1976 was very much less than appearances suggested. The seemingly rapid growth of the National Enterprise Board was entirely due to the simple transfer of already existing government shareholdings from the Department of Industry in Victoria Street London SW1 to the offices of the NEB round the corner in Grosvenor Gardens, SW1. British Leyland contributed 191,000 and Rolls Royce a further 62,000 to the NEB's quarter of a million employees. In the same manoeuvre the Board 'acquired' other existing state-owned firms such as ICL, Ferranti and Alfred Herbert.

Table 2 **The pattern of the National Enterprise Board's holdings** (at 28 September 1979)

Company	% of all shares and loans
BL Ltd	67.7
Rolls Royce Ltd	19.3
ICL Ltd	0.9
Ferranti	0.5
Alfred Herbert	3.3
'Entrepreneurial'	8.3

Source: National Enterprise Board, Interim Report for six months to 30 June 1979.

As Table 2 shows these five firms accounted for 92 per cent of all the share and loan capital invested by the NEB in 1979. Less than 8 per cent of its assets were committed to genuinely 'entrepreneurial' activity. This was a far cry from the dynamic industrial leadership promised. Something had been lost in the construction of the NEB. What was missing was the commitment to move into profitable manufacturing with new forms of public ownership. An NEB dominated by BL and Rolls could hardly be accused of 'directly harnessing mesoeconomic power', to use Stuart Holland's expression, for bringing oligopoly under social control.

After the event it became common knowledge that the NEB proposal had never commanded the support of the parliamentary Labour Party's leadership. As soon as appearances respectably permitted, Harold Wilson was eager to ditch the whole baggage of the wide-ranging intervention implied by the new planning framework. With splits in Labour's hierarchy and a campaign launched by business against the new model, it became easy for senior civil servants to pick off the proposed measures as well as the odd minister. By the time Tony Benn found himself Harold Wilson's hostage to business confidence, it was too late for the Labour left to succeed in whipping up grass-roots support for Labour's programme. After Benn was removed from industry to energy, relatively little was heard of harnessing the forces of oligopoly to serve the social interest.

It was hard to believe that the National Enterprise Board and planning agreement system of 1976 was in any way related to the original 1973 proposals, such was the transformation that had taken place. Stuart Holland and others had originally conceived of a state holding company managing 25 of the top 100 manufacturing firms. At the end of the day the NEB's largest 'conquest' was BL. In fact, the moment that BL was delivered up to the NEB, the character of the latter as some kind of casualty station for ailing enterprise was as good as set. Stuart Holland and others had always intended that for the NEB to work properly it had to be mainly involved in profitable manufacturing. Their view was that BL should be dealt with by the government quite separately from the new dynamic and profitable public enterprise they were recommending. As it turned out the largest firms on the NEB's books were enormous loss-makers.

Given the size of the task placed before the original idea of the enterprise board, it was essential that appropriate finance be made available so that purchases of the right firms, in the right sectors, if need be by compulsion, could be made. However, the Labour government saw fit to give the NEB a spending limit of only £700 million in the first instance, later raised to £1,000 million. It was hardly the sort of money that would give the Board a free hand to search the private sector for suitable subsidiaries. The government also submitted to business pressure by disallowing any compulsory acquisition.

Originally, between and 100 and 150 planning agreements had been envisaged with other non-NEB large firms. The power to force firms into making the agreements should also have existed. Again, bowing to the pressure of private capital, Wilson ditched this element of the planning. In fact only one such agreement was ever concluded in the private sector and that was in 1975 with Chrysler, a firm in receipt of huge state aid, after its management had threatened the complete shut-down of its UK operations. Holland and others had hoped that new forms of planning would introduce greater democracy in the plant. But even in NEB firms themselves, no real workers' plan was ever drawn up. Yet, the flow of public funds to companies in difficulty or need, inside and outside the NEB, continued unabated. Time and again, Labour left-wingers Audrey Wise and Jeff Rooker pressed the Secretary of State to make access to government funds contingent upon the introduction of planning agreements. Equally often the reply came from the Department of Industry that it was *not* government policy to make aid conditional in that manner.

Because of the deepening economic crisis, the government increasingly found itself playing the role of benefactor to ailing industries. Ever larger sums were handed out to private enterprise in a vast panoply of state aids. During the life of the last Labour government, around £15,000 million was allocated through schemes like regional development grants, temporary employment subsidies, youth opportunities, accelerated investment projects and subsidies to small firms. In this context the NEB's £1,000 million was peripheral to the needs of private capital. In any case most of this was swallowed up by BL and Rolls Royce. The Enterprise Board invested less than £100 million over its five-year life in profitable sectors of industry. And, surprisingly perhaps, the chief characteristic of most government aid to industry was how few strings were attached. Little was demanded in return for the state's generosity. It was not used to obtain an ownership stake in private enterprise, not even for the much less radical purpose of levering firms into planning agreements with unions and government.

In the grand design of 1973 the state holding company was supposed, by its example and the force of its weight in the economy, to mould the behaviour of manufacturers at large. In reality the National Enterprise Board, because of its small stake in profitable manufacturing, had no influence over other producers. Indeed, it seemed to be more susceptible to the influence of private business than the other way round. In tackling its own restructuring problems it adopted the same solutions as any private capitalist would have done. This was a reversal of dramatic proportions. In following orthodox market-type solutions in revamping its own business, the NEB completely overlooked the duty it had been given to generate employment. It joined the great British job shake-out with as much vigour as the next capitalist enterprise. One commentator writing in the financial press wryly and accurately noted, 'the chief impact of the NEB on employment in the North West has been BL's closure at Speke'.

Workers quickly noticed the surprising job loss in state-owned firms. This was deeply disturbing since workers expected a Labour government to behave in a fundamentally different way from private capitalists. Was the theory of the state as entrepreneur to be taken literally, in perhaps a nineteenth-century sense – when each individual firm had to shape up to market discipline or go under? Public ownership offered no job protection superior to that of the market generally.

Take the motor industry in which the state, through BL, was heavily involved. As plans for BL's future development seemed to offer little, a workers' enquiry was set up into the motor industry to make sense of what was going on. One clear conclusion was that 'state intervention in the motor industry in the current crisis has reinforced rather than reversed the harsh forces of reorganisation at the expense of the workforce'.

Or take another ailing sector in which the state had become heavily involved in the 1970s – machine tools. The Coventry Machine Tools Workers' Committee organised a similar investigation to that of colleagues in motors, again to discover what was going in their industry. Their conclusions were identical: 'state financial aid seems to have actually assisted the reorganisation and rationalisation of the industry along purely commercial lines rather than put it on a different footing'.

As for the NEB, they commented:

> [it] does not challenge the commercial independence or priorities of the firms it owns, and in the case of the Speke and Tress closures, rejected representations to intervene from workers with alternative proposals for these companies.

These alternatives will be looked at more closely in the last chapter.

But all of this surely made a strange turn of events. A Labour government elected on a strongly interventionist manifesto had promised socialist transformation. No one thought this would happen overnight, but people did expect to see some progress. In practice Labour's major economic intervention was limited to merely doling out to an ailing manufacturing industry large sums of money with few strings attached. Where state ownership existed it was, as always, predominantly in companies that had become unprofitable. What was even more surprising, when state companies showed signs of restored profitability, it seemed that the government wanted to return them to their former habitat in the private sector.

Now, the Thatcher government believes in 'disengaging' the state from the economy. For Margaret Thatcher and Keith Joseph the NEB *was* the casualty ward for infirm enterprise. When firms recovered they left the hospital for the bracing winds of free competition. There is some semblance of an economic philosophy in this Conservative doctrine. But what is one to make of a Labour government which gets its National Enterprise Board to sell off its prize assets, as it did with a portion of its Ferranti shares in 1978?

The fund of optimism and enthusiasm of workers who really believed in the 1974 Labour government as a vehicle of socialist change was shattered by 1979. Where the Labour government was generously handing out cash to the private sector, it only had prevarication and confusion ready for the workers who went to it for help.

Perhaps most shabbily treated were the workers from Vickers' Scotswood plant on Tyneside and those from Lucas Aerospace. In earlier years, shortly after the 1974 election, it had been possible for workers to get in touch directly with industry ministers. Tony Benn and Eric Heffer did give some encouragement to the idea, for example, of worker co-operatives, whatever their later weaknesses turned out to be. By the time the Vickers management announced their plans to close down Scotswood, and Lucas its intended large-scale redundancies, a much less approachable Gerald Kaufman had been installed as industry minister. No matter how the workers fought the closures – whether by occupying, by setting up combine organisations to fight more effectively throughout the whole firm, or by pointing to socially useful products they could be making instead of drawing dole – they found an unexpectedly cool reception at the Department of Industry.

From the story of Labour's attempt to plan over the mid- to late 1970s, two different conclusions can be drawn. One says that there is something basically faulty with the idea of the state as entrepreneur as it was put forward. This is the conclusion that many workers now accept, and which was clearly stated by the Liverpool delegate to the recently organised workers' enquiry into the NEB. For him the lesson was 'you cannot plan what you do not control and you cannot control what you do not own.' This conclusion strikes at the very heart of the case put forward by Stuart Holland, which asserted that selective public ownership backed up by planning agreements could deliver sufficient control to transform the capitalist economy.

The other lesson often drawn, in particular by the parliamentary leaders of the Labour left, is quite simply that the planning policies advocated in 1973 were never properly implemented. They are still to be tested. To put them to the test what is needed is a strong leadership, one that is genuinely committed to socialism. Democratisation of the party is seen as an essential step in producing an accountable leadership which can be called to task for ignoring the manifesto. The new procedure for the election of the party leader is an important step forward in this respect.

The greater democracy of the Labour Party in the early 1980s has also had the effect of frightening off the worst kind of right-wing Labour politicians (mostly into the arms of the SDP). The party is better off without these MPs who are afraid of mandatory reselection. But with the focus of attention so sharply on internal affairs, not enough consideration has been given to external matters such as the opposition of private business to the 1974 planning proposals. Yet that opposition broke their back.

Big business mugs the government

The publication of Labour's programme in 1973 provided the initial frightener to the business community. With the election of a Labour government, it seemed to be only a matter of time before manifesto promises would become policy. Proposals to take over 25 top firms and to introduce compulsory planning agreements with others made private capital exceedingly nervous. The CBI's view was that it 'regarded as non-negotiable any attempt to subject the leading 100 companies to a planning agreements system'. It went on to raise the spectre that government policies 'would involve an extension of state ownership never yet experienced in this or any other liberal democratic society'.

The publication of the 1974 White Paper, *The Regeneration of British Industry*, did nothing to overcome the anxieties of private capital. True, the proposal to nationalise some 25 major companies had disappeared and planning agreements were to be purely voluntary. But, at the same time, some sort of commitment to extend public ownership in new directions into private manufacturing seemed to remain. The Tory Party went on the offensive with their industry spokesperson, Michael Heseltine, darkly claiming that Labour was only trying to disguise its true intentions in the White Paper but 'this would not deceive the electorate'. With unusual perception he pointed out that 'if the government is to achieve its purpose, it will need to enmesh the largest and most successful companies . . . the very companies least in need of help'. He had nothing to worry about. The government no longer really wanted to bring to life the kind of enterprise board that had been discussed in 1973.

The attack mounted by business and its representatives in and around parliament against Labour's interventionist plan was well organised. The press mounted a campaign of extraordinary vilification against the industry minister, Tony Benn. In the imagination of the gutter press there was nothing to distinguish the strange new creed of 'Bennery' from the slightly better-known Russian Bolshevism. Heseltine toured the country to whip up anti-government feeling, lecturing under the banner, 'Great Britain not State Britain'. Prominent industrialists, including the heads of ICI, Pilkingtons and the Imperial Group, spoke out against the White Paper suggestions. The head of Unilever described its proposals as 'sufficiently vague to be sinister'. ICI went as far as spending £60,000 in writing to shareholders, employees and those on company pensions explaining why it should not be allowed to become one of the big private sector firms which might be bought by the NEB.

The short fuse to this explosion of protest lay in the threatened extension of state ownership and control over *profitable* industrial sectors. No post-war government had ever attempted to draw profitable firms into the public sector to the extent threatened in 1973. The unwritten rules that roughly delineate the proportions of private and public control of resources in a capitalist economy had hitherto been respected by governments. But the 1973 announcement by the Labour Party, albeit while in opposition, that it intended to change the rules of the game was unprecedented. Antique commitments to extend public ownership given in the most general spirit could be comfortably discounted by capital as part of Labour Party mythology, necessary to placate sections of the membership, but of no real importance and posing no danger to private interest. The crucial difference between, say, clause four of the party constitution and the most recent planning proposals was that the proposed instruments of state intervention were now specific and fully described in advance.

From Labour's viewpoint this specification of planning instruments was a major step forward on the 1960s approach to the national plan. It was thought then that announcing growth targets would be enough. Private business would fall in with government plans and 4 per cent growth per annum would become a self-fulfilling prophecy. That of course did not happen. For Labour an important lesson seemed to have been learned. It was that effective planning needs appropriate planning instruments.

One obvious worry for capital was that the new rules of the economic management game gave no clear limit to the state's role. It might 'only' be 25 firms to start with but why should it stop there? Intervening to correct the failures of markets (for example, preventing monopolies from abusing their position) is one thing, but an 'entrepreneurial state' is something quite different, and for capital, quite unacceptable. The 'market failure' tradition of intervention is tolerable because its bounds are well defined. The new planning proposals had no such limits. It was the thin end of the socialist wedge.

Something of the same problem had been met by the Attlee government in its troubles over steel nationalisation in 1951. That, too, had succeeded in whipping up the hostility of capital. The owners mounted 'a full-scale propaganda campaign' against the proposals. Their friends in the Conservative Party helped by organising parliamentary delaying tactics. And again the reason for this opposition was that, as noted earlier, sections of the industry were profitable and indistinguishable from manufacturing generally. As

Doug McEachern put it in his *Capital and Class* article, 'the Labour government's move to nationalise steel pushed at the limits of the logic behind the construction of a state owned base of a mixed economy.'

The resistance of business to state involvement in profitable manufacturing is not just a British phenomenon. In Italy, where after all the NEB idea came from, the same factor helps to explain the small size of the Italian IRI. There is even acknowledgement of this from Stuart Holland in his influential book, *The Socialist Challenge*, published in 1975. He explains away the reluctance of the authorities to use the IRI more vigorously by pointing to the fact that 'public enterprise in profitable manufacturing is an implicit challenge to competing private enterprise.' The challenge is actually quite explicit and not only to 'competing enterprise', but what is surprising in arguments for state entrepreneurship is that little is made of the resistance bound to meet the proposals, or the steps that need to be taken to counter it.

Some notable facts are worth reciting in this context. The Italian IRI accounts for something of the order of 6 per cent of manufacturing employment and it has not been able to grow significantly beyond this in an almost 50-year life span. The British NEB was originally designed to take up around 20 per cent of manufacturing employment. Building such a large state sector from scratch is bound to cause political problems as capital resists the move. Yet these problems have very rarely been examined by those who formulated Labour's new planning machinery in the early 1970s.

While one can understand why business mobilised against Labour's programme, it still remains puzzling that neither Labour government nor trade unions saw fit to build any popular support for planning. Little attempt was made to explain to workers the content of the party's planning ideas. Probably very few people outside a small circle around Benn and Holland had a clear idea of what all the fuss was about in the press of 1974. The lack of discussion on the issues gave the impression that Labour was committed to what was essentially a technocratic planning model, one to be implemented by those experts who were lucky enough to have a scientific understanding of the nature of oligopoly. This may not have been intended by the leaders of the Labour left, but, unfortunately, it was what was seen in practice.

4.

Towards a Socialist Plan for Britain

Planning and the next Labour government

In the early 1970s Labour Party economic policy seemed simply to appear as if by magic. Few people were familiar with the process of policy-making and even fewer with the policies themselves. The greatest interest in Labour's socialist challenge seemed to come from financial journalists. One or two academics also found interesting ideas to contemplate in Labour Party policy.

As more time passed it became clear that the CBI was a far better publicist of the proposed socialist planning than either the Labour Party or trades unions. The CBI was actively persuading its members, its political representatives, and the general public of the dangers in store if the Labour government started any economic planning. Meanwhile, we can only suppose that both unions and Labour Party assumed their members would understand the new directions in economic policy through some kind of socialist intuition. But there was no socialist telepathy and Labour's economic programme remained unanchored in the workplace or local community. It was therefore to be expected that it could be easily swept away. And indeed the tempest of business opposition was more than enough to sink the good ship 'state entrepreneur'.

In the early 1980s, again with Labour in opposition, economic policies have emerged in an altogether different and healthier manner. First, there has been a genuine attempt to encourage wide debate within the party. Second, the Labour Party has joined in a fruitful policy-making partnership with the TUC, through the forum of the liaison committee originally set up in the early 1970s to ward off Edward Heath's attack on the unions. Clearly written pamphlets have appeared describing the labour movement's alternative to Thatcherism. Through continuing discussion these have evolved into a full set of proposals towards building a socialist plan for Britain.

A third point worth noting concerns the economic initiatives taken in the early months of 1982 by some local authorities intent on contributing to a truly practical socialist economics. The GLC in London and the West Midlands and Sheffield councils are trying to show the relevance of a socialist economic policy *even* while the Tories still pursue slump economics at the national level. These experiments have their roots in the experiences of the 1970s which saw, as well as the defeat of government economic planning, the encouraging emergence of workers' plans. Among the latter, the Lucas plan, which proposed socially useful production when management threatened redundancy, is best known.

Political change within the Labour Party has also helped to make policy-making more reliant on public discussion. If, in the early 1980s, there is more accountability within the Labour Party, making the atmosphere a distinctly healthier one than in the 1970s, what can be said about the content of policy? Compared to the seventies there are some very clear improvements. The main one, apart from the style of policy formulation, is that economic and industrial policies form a coherent package.

This package has been encapsulated in what is known as the alternative economic strategy (AES). There are various versions of what such a policy could be but all rest essentially on three pillars. First, there has to be increased spending in the economy in order to reduce unemployment. Second, this has to be done behind the protection of import controls, which is seen as the only way of avoiding a balance of payments crisis. Third, spending must be well directed within the economy, that is, some form of economic planning is required to ensure that spending reaches the 'right' sectors.

The AES has been the subject of much debate and the discussion here will only take up those elements that relate to the theme of this book. What kind of planning framework is envisaged in Labour's alternative?

'Economic planning and industrial democracy'

Central to the new planning is that things should be done as the result of mutual agreement between government, trade unions and employers. Investment, location, price and other policies of large private firms will, it is hoped, be heavily influenced by government through disbursement of public funds. Private business will be financially induced to make its development plans blend harmoniously with the intentions of government. Ultimately, the sanction also exists of public ownership where managements seem to follow a too obstructive path. The device that will embody the tripartite planning settlement in individual cases is the so-called development plan for the firm.

The government will also have a direct hand in the future of important industries through extended public ownership, which will give it a presence in each key sector. It must be said though that there is still some old-fashioned ambiguity about the appropriate rate and extent of nationalisation in future planning policy. A mix of direct control and indirect control through the development plans of private firms will constitute the main instruments of economic planning.

There is a great deal of similarity between 'agreed development plans' and the earlier 'planning agreements'. But there is one crucial difference. It seems that in the early eighties there is a much greater Labour Party commitment to make use of the revamped planning agreements. Perhaps some evidence of a greater enthusiasm for planning can be seen in the careful preparation that has gone into laying the institutional framework to support the system of 'agreed development plans'. The major innovation in this respect will be the establishment of a completely new government department – the Department of Economic and Industrial Planning – which will negotiate and conclude the agreements with individual companies.

This department will also build a medium-term plan that looks five years ahead and it will ensure that short-term agreements are consistent with longer-run objectives. Apart from the broad aims upon which a socialist government might be elected, the raw material for this plan-building would seem to flow from two major directions. First, a national planning council will be set up as an independent body but with the tripartite (government, management and unions) constitution of the present National Economic Development Office – Neddy as it is popularly known. The council is likely to have similar functions to Neddy, that is, it will help to identify bottlenecks to economic expansion, encourage adoption of better practice and techniques among firms, and so on. Second, the government will hope to conduct, together with unions and employers, a national economic assessment that will look at overall goals, priorities and distributional issues. These independent bodies will, in some way that is not altogether clear, fuel the government planning department, which will in turn transform broad intentions into the concrete reality of the new-style planning agreements.

Not only do planning agreements reappear in a new shape in 1982 but there is also some similarity between the Department of Economic and Industrial Planning and the Department of Economic Affairs which was set up by the 1964 Wilson government, also to oversee the construction and implementation of a national plan. The critical difference intended in the new model is that the planning department should have real power where the DEA had none. Thus, the planning department will, it is argued, entice and cajole and finally push private companies into acting in the spirit of government economic policy via the agreed development plan. For this to happen successfully there must clearly be one, and only one, identifiable source of governmental power in economic policy matters. Obviously the planning department must wield that power.

This arrangement has radical implications for the traditional role of the Chancellor of the Exchequer and the supporting staff at the Treasury. In the new set up, the Treasury may just as well be dissolved and replaced by a small department of book-keepers who will ensure that state funds are not misappropriated. It seems however that in Labour's plans the Treasury is still to have an existence, though without any control over macroeconomic policy. With respective roles clearly stated, it is hoped to avoid the tensions that arose in the past between planning bodies and Treasury, which were so destructive to the former.

The thread of continuity from the industrial policies of the 1970s leads to an invigorated National Enterprise Board in the new planning model. The basis for this is the view that the NEB was never tested during 1974–79 and it has an important role in plan implementation as the government's direct link with industrial life. The NEB will be set up by, and report to, the Department of Economic and Industrial Planning. The Department will also breathe life into an idea first suggested by G.D.H.Cole in the

1930s by setting up a National Investment Bank, which will channel funds for long-term investment to selected industrial sectors. In order to facilitate the smooth operation of the planning process, new skills will have to be acquired by all those involved – trade unionists, civil servants and cabinet ministers. A National Planning College will be established to fulfil this educational and training role. It is likely that the inspiration for this comes from the reputation of the French polytechnic institutions, noted for the professionalism with which they have equipped all those who have participated in indicative planning over the years.

So, one can see that no stone seems to have been left unturned in the search by the Labour Party and TUC for a socialist planning model. The main planning instruments are to be the planning agreements, which will give the authorities indirect control over private firms together with direct control, through the NEB, over an enlarged state-owned sector. Institutions will be founded at central government level to give the plan the muscle and back up it needs. Training will be available in the new Planning College to acquaint people with planning skills.

The Labour Party also proposes to enact legislation which will improve the access of working people to company information. One step it hopes will immediately improve the flow of information is the demand that major company decisions be notified to the workforce well in advance, and that a 60-day period of grace be given before any action is taken by management. The 60 days is to allow workers to respond with counter-proposals should management's intentions be considered unsatisfactory. After that, an agreement will have to be reached between interested parties. How exactly this is to happen is not made clear at present.

There are annoying ambiguities of the sort already mentioned in the planning proposals but some things are reasonably clear. We can see that a planning system is being suggested which will be concerned with institutional change and also with the extension of democracy at the plant level. It also seems that official policy has made a welcome move away from the technocratic approach to planning of both the 1960s Department of Economic Affairs and the 1970s industrial strategy.

Can it work?

The alternative economic strategy is in better shape today than was the case a decade ago. But the planning system advocated at present is sufficiently similar to the old industrial strategy to make us wonder if the same fate may not await it. This question has also been raised by the National Executive Committee (NEC) of the Labour Party. In the pamphlet, *The Socialist Alternative*, published in 1981, an answer is given. Its substance is that the previous strategy failed because of

> the lack of follow-through from sectoral plans to company level action. There was no leverage over the investment plans of the major companies in each sector . . . and too little public investment.

Now it is obvious that 'follow-through' is seriously intended in the 1982 proposals. 'Leverage' should also be secured through a much larger NEB and the force of 'agreed development plans'. The problem is that even a road paved with good intentions may not lead us to the desired destination. There is clearly a deeper obstruction to a socialist plan for Britain: it is the resistance of business to greater public ownership and control of private industry. Unfortunately, there is inadequate recognition of this in the Labour Party's otherwise plausible planning suggestions.

The Labour Party NEC is convinced that 'big companies have had a shattering experience under the Tory government.' The example of ICI is cited as a typical casualty, forced by government policy into announcing its first ever losses. So while the Labour Party can acknowledge that 'some big companies will make political objections to Labour's plans', they will none the less have 'good business reasons' for welcoming the proposed planning framework. This is a refrain that is becoming increasingly accepted as a plain truth by sections of the labour movement. Take for example the claim made in Labour's well-produced pamphlet, *Britain on the Dole*, published in early 1982, that 'these plans will be a great help for companies because they will provide a firm basis for companies to draw up their own plans'.

Some industrial and economic commentators have also detected, in the way labour leaders discuss planning, a desire to convince business that the new policies would serve it well. The labour editor of the *Financial Times* was able to begin a report (on 11 May 1982) with the sentence: 'The TUC yesterday claimed that the plans it has developed jointly with the Labour Party were more in managers' interest than were the Government's policies'.

This desire to please on the part of the Labour Party is likely to become an ever more popular tune, particularly as the run up to any election starts. The great danger to socialist policies is that if big business starts to call the tune then that is likely to be the end of those policies. Admittedly Harold Wilson may have been more eager than Michael Foot or Tony Benn to oblige private industry, but this approach to winning support for the new planning is an extremely treacherous one. Is a TUC that refuses to mount any serious campaign against unemployment and the deterioration in working conditions likely to mount much of a defence of socialist economic planning should management seek changes to the original policy?

The extent to which the Labour Party and TUC are prepared to underplay business resistance to socialist plans is nowhere more strikingly revealed than in a recent document entitled *Economic Issues Facing the Next Labour Government*. Its aim is explicitly to examine the policies that will be needed,

> to assure that expansion is not frustrated – as it has been so often in the past – by such constraints as import penetration and outflow of capital, inflation or shortages of skilled labour.

The big surprise is that the business hostility that smashed Labour's 1974 industrial policies is not directly mentioned at all. Yet the element of that strategy that private capital found most unacceptable, the commitment to 'establish a publicly owned stake in *each* important sector of industry' (my emphasis), is reiterated with renewed vigour.

Another surprise, which augurs extremely ill for the future of any socialist planning, was that, in the 1982 ASLEF dispute, the TUC accepted the government's view on the necessity for ASLEF to abandon the guaranteed eight-hour day. Even before the ASLEF strike and during the health service dispute, a *Financial Times* editorial declared, on 25 June 1982,

> As has been widely noted and resented in private industry, the pains of disinflation were at first quite largely restricted to the private sector. More recently, the Government has been prepared to confront some very costly disputes to impose a similar constraint on the civil service and now on the health service. . . . Public sector industries . . . like private industry, also need to make some painful and long delayed changes in working practice to achieve higher efficiency.

Do these sound like opinions likely to be won over to the view that socialist planning is in fact in management's interest? It is surely over-optimistic to believe that the 'political objections' to Labour's plans are likely to be as limited as is implicitly suggested in *Economic Issues Facing the Next Labour Government*. The plain fact of the matter is that Thatcherism has strengthened the power of management. There seems to be a poor understanding among some labour leaders of the very real advantages offered to management by Thatcherism. Wages can be held down; workers can be disciplined. A director of one Birmingham engineering company explained to journalists of the *Sunday Times* early in 1982 what this meant:

> The T&GWU and the AUEW had enormous power here on the shop floor . . . but the redundancies have got rid of the troublemakers who came to power in the 1960s. We've taken out 30 of them who were like a cancer.

How would the Labour Party persuade that director that his real self-interest lay in the enthusiastic embracing of socialist planning?

Surely it is clear that there are two distinct ideas that do not fit together. One is the logic imposed by the pursuit of private profit and the other is the logic of social need. The former is reasonably well served by Thatcherism, despite the real difficulties faced by some business people; the latter by socialist planning. There is no common ground between them. The argument for socialist planning has to be won among working people in Britain, not among their employers. The main weakness of the Labour Party–TUC planning schemes is that they do not make up their minds which logic they want to follow. There is talk about rejecting the anarchy of the market and instead planning for social needs. But at the same time there is the hint, in the way policies are publicly presented, that management may also be pleasantly accommodated in a new wing of the planning house.

There is evidently a real danger that socialist policies will be 'adjusted' in the future in the style of the 1973–75 period. Perhaps one source of this danger lies in the Labour Party rush to embrace French and Japanese planning ideas. These are used in argument to show that successful capitalist economies often succeed because of deliberate acts of government intervention. They also help to counter the staunch pro-market ideology of the high priests and priestess of the Tory party. But what is sometimes overlooked is the fact that France and Japan offer instances of successful *capital-*

ist planning. It is perhaps surprising that the TUC should also have neglected the fact that French trade unionists often choose not to sit at the places offered them round the indicative planning table.

Current planning proposals are weakened by the neglect of capitalist resistance. But it is also true that there can be no socialist planning without popular support. Another weakness of the planning on offer is that, as it stands, it is not capable of winning enough support among working people and the unemployed. This is because not enough of a break has been made with past attempts to plan and with the market logic that elevates 'competitiveness' and 'efficiency' as the highest and most worthy objectives of economic endeavour. The issues are very closely interlinked, as past attempts by Labour governments to plan have shown. In particular the period 1974–79 saw public institutions, the flag bearers of the industrial strategy, conduct an industrial restructuring indistinguishable in its effects on employment from that of purely private sector firms. The NEB presided over massive redundancies. Trade unionists were naturally bitterly disappointed. This is why the reception for the new planning is likely to be cool where it matters most of all – in the workplace. The crucial issue – where socialist planning for social need should stand in relation to competitiveness – is something we will clearly have to return to.

So, can the planning system recently put forward by the Labour Party and TUC work? If political life were a game played according to accepted rules and diligently umpired to ensure sporting behaviour, then the planning system would have life breathed into it the day after a Labour election victory at the polls. Some technical problems might emerge; in such a system they would surely prove amenable to solution, provided the umpire could ensure the maintenance of goodwill. There could be some kind of arbitration over difficulties caused by petty jealousy (say, between the Treasury and planning department). Disagreements over income distribution could be similarly handled by a super-Advisory, Conciliation and Arbitration Service. Planning would be viewed as a rational process by which intelligent people managed economic and social affairs.

It is, however, unlikely to turn out like this in the immediate future. The right to private profits will be jealously guarded by those who do well out of the present system. Planning – the replacement of private by social decision-making – will be viewed as a threat by management, as will any extended state ownership of profitable private industry. As it stands, present planning policies are likely to collapse into some form of controlled capitalist management along what is known as corporate state lines. Private interests will come to dominate the planning department in the way they dominated British wartime planning, the Japanese ministry for international trade and industry, the French plan or, more recently, the Labour government's NEB.

There is another possibility though: that the logic of the market is firmly rejected, the hostility of private business is openly accepted and that arguments in favour of planning for social need are unashamedly developed among working and unemployed people. To do this in a convincing way, the two contrasting ideas mentioned must be met head on. We need to show how the idea of social need can be unfolded to build an economics of common sense. If Margaret Thatcher can persuade large numbers of people that economic success comes with maintaining unemployment at well over three million, then surely our task in developing a practical economics of social need cannot be too burdensome.

Workers' initiatives – need, not profit

The possibility that the route to efficiency defined by market forces might creep back into the alternative economic strategy and its planning arrangements is worrying. Yet many people believe misguidedly, though for quite understandable reasons, that there is no alternative to the rigours of market discipline. It is frequently argued that to attempt to make choices in any more open and deliberate manner will lead simply to an overdeveloped and stifling bureaucracy which is often said to be the penalty in playing the planning game, and again to look at East Europe all this seems unquestionable truth.

In the economies which are at present centrally planned there is indeed no democracy, but this lack is precisely the greatest internal obstacle to the improved economic performance desperately needed East of the Elbe. Productivity is held back by the overcentralised procedures for economic decision-making. For socialists the lesson is clear. The only worthwhile planning is democratic planning. In Poland during the recent 18 months of open discussion, it seemed that many had drawn the same conclusion. The focus of debate was on how to democratise Polish planning, not on how it might be possible to reintroduce some elements of capitalism (see chapter two).

The most encouraging initiatives towards building a democratic planning system have not come from Poland or Hungary nor even from Japan or France in recent years. Instead our own experience, here in Britain, gives us much to build on. This is not, of course, a reference to the record of the Wilson government. The crucial initiatives in the 1970s have come from workers who have often ingeniously responded to management's redundancy threats. Not all of these initiatives have been immediately successful, but they do begin to show us what the alternative logic to the pursuit of private profits actually means. They begin at least to suggest that competitiveness may be secured by creating, rather than destroying, jobs.

Lucas

Lucas is an extremely large company operating in many countries throughout the Western world. In the 1970s international competition 'forced' rationalisation on the firm and this in turn led 'inevitably' to plant closure and redundancies in the UK. People were to be thrown out of work for the greater 'efficiency' of the company. The pursuit of maximum profits is the motto of Lucas Industries and if this means relocating production away from the UK then so be it. The social costs imposed on ex-Lucas employees, their families and others indirectly affected by plant closures must all be accepted, not by Lucas of course, but by society as a whole. All of this is eminently reasonable in the logic of the maximisation of private profits. It was, however, not acceptable to Lucas employees.

The story of the Lucas workers' fight for jobs has been told elsewhere and the briefest summary will serve our present purposes. Their response to the threat of job losses was to ask a very simple question. What social needs existed that Lucas workers, with their particular skills, could easily satisfy? Of course there were many. In a company-wide questionnaire no fewer than 150 socially useful products were suggested. Of these, 12 were chosen for detailed study and incorporation in the alternative plan put to management by Lucas workers. They believed that their plan was an exceptionally strong card to play against management's closure threats, especially in view of the existence of a Labour government committed, it seemed, to the idea of planning agreements and trade-union participation in company decision-making. Lucas management was, however, completely uninterested in the ideas in the workers' plan. The government had surprisingly little enthusiasm either; the end result was government aid to the company in return for the meagre undertaking that it would axe fewer jobs than it had originally intended.

The importance of the alternative plan was that it was a workers' plan. It was a classic example of planning from the 'bottom up'. It showed that trade unionists could devise an alternative, socially responsible development path for a large company hitherto intent solely on maximising profit. Furthermore, despite the fact that Lucas is a huge firm, this plan was drawn up in a democratic manner. It was a plan that workers within the firm found easy to identify with. It was a plan of historic importance.

The motor industry

There is probably no other industry as sharply competitive as motors. This is a sector dominated by a few enormous firms which operate on a world scale. International competition has led to the production of the 'world car' whereby each major firm organises the production of certain models on a worldwide basis. Assembly takes place in one or two key locations, strategically placed close to important markets. Different components are produced across many different countries, each chosen to contribute best to the corporate goal of profit maximisation.

The same logic has led motor firms operating in Britain to close plants in favour of streamlined production in countries where labour may be cheaper and/or more amenable to company discipline. The inability of British Leyland to compete successfully has led to plant closures. The Speke Triumph factory in May 1978 was the most notorious example of state-owned industry behaving exactly like a private capitalist concern. The fact that a Labour government was installed in Whitehall seemed not to matter one iota. Competitiveness, in BL's case, dictated a 'slimming down' in the interests of cutting losses rather than making profits. Plants could be closed, skills lost at enormous social cost even in state-owned firms.

Was this inevitable? Shop stewards thought not and have argued before the Ryder enquiry into BL that the problem of the industry was lack of investment. What was needed therefore was a 'planned capital investment programme supported by public funds' under 'full democratic control'. Under Michael Edwardes, BL has been more intent on waging a war on organised labour in order to win back for management the unquestioned right to manage regardless of consequences for employees or society as a whole.

The Chrysler crisis of the mid-1970s is particularly interesting. It was usual for the firm's financial problems to be blamed on competition and an unobliging workforce. In reality Chrysler UK was suffering from a chronic lack of investment. For years the company had been shifting production to more 'obliging' locations, for example, South America. There is also some reason to believe that it had been engaged in the transfer-pricing game, by which multinational companies making profits in high tax countries shift them to tax havens by charging subsidiaries there artificially low export prices. In the Chrysler case it seemed that profits made in the UK often ended up in Switzerland to the obvious detriment of investment and jobs in the UK.

Clearly an alternative plan could have been devised to that dictated by the quest for maximum profits. In fact Chrysler shop stewards did produce such a plan, which spelt out what investment would be needed for survival, and what sort of alternative products could be manufactured to satisfy social needs. Chrysler management was plainly uninterested in all this. Their concern was solely with getting the maximum government hand-out. They achieved this. With £169 million of state funds they could still lose another 8,000 jobs, even with a Labour government in office.

Workers in the motor industry were the victims of often sensational capital restructuring throughout the 1970s. To make sense of what was happening, workers from Chrysler, Vauxhall, Ford and BL launched an enquiry into the industry in 1976. They concluded that there was

> a wide range of alternative transport vehicles which the industry could diversify into, which could be made by the existing work force with existing skills and technology, and which better meet our society's transport needs than the current range of private motor vehicles.

These ranged from invalid cars, the Lucas worker's road/rail vehicle, to improved taxi design. Is the alternative logic to mass redundancy an implausible one? No. In the words of the workers:

> the stumbling block to a relatively secure and socially useful

> vehicle industry is not lack of ideas or plans for the use of existing capacity – rather what is missing is the harnessing of political strength . . . The problems to be overcome, therefore, are not technical but political.

Machine tools

Job loss in this sector has also been immense in the UK in the 1970s. According to the employers that is the unfortunate by-product of 'slimming for profitability' which in turn is, they say, the key to survival. Trade unionists have been reluctant to accept this as a satisfactory explanation of what has been happening in the industry. The Coventry Machine Tools Workers' Committee inaugurated its own study of what was going on. They found, as in motors, a distinct lack of any willingness of management to invest.

There were also some very peculiar things happening to profits that had been made in the 'better' times. For example, during 1965–70 Alfred Herbert, a leading producer, recorded a total profit of £8.7 million and over the same period distributed £9.2 million in dividends to shareholders. Profits were simply being sucked out of the industry with nothing being ploughed back to secure its future. Then, when a lack of markets led to an intensified international competition in the 1970s, workers were asked to shoulder the entire burden. Another instance of private decision-making with huge social consequences, particularly for geographical areas strongly dependent on their machine tool industries for jobs.

Coventry workers saw things differently from management. They had no doubt that

> a plan can be developed, as it was by the Lucas Aerospace Shop Stewards' Combine Committee, out of a wide public discussion about the kinds of products which are socially necessary and useful and which can be produced by machine tool workers, but which are not adequately provided under a system of private ownership of industry geared to the maximisation of profit.

Among the immediate steps which it was hoped the Labour government might have taken, it was suggested that any machine tool concern trying to shed jobs should lose all government support. Workers argued that if firms could be penalised for breaking government pay restraint policy, then the same should hold for employment policy. The government was also asked to take initial steps in developing an industry-wide plan by co-ordinating the machine tool purchases of all nationalised industries. In the longer term, with state support, especially research support, a plan for socially useful products should have been aimed at. There was no alternative plan in this sector as well worked out as that at Lucas, but with the backing of the Labour government is could easily have been produced.

Vickers Scotswood

The Scotswood mechanical engineering plant may have been a fairly small star in the constellation owned by Vickers but at least it seemed to be fairly successful. Throughout the 1970s a small profit was regularly made and in 1977 the plant even won the Vickers group award for export performance. It was something of a rude surprise for Scotswood workers to discover, shortly after, that Vickers' head office wanted the plant closed down. As might be expected management's explanation for this was a typical and seemingly unchallengeable reference to 'tough market conditions', a 'lack of demand' for Scotswood's traditional products, leading 'inevitably' to the 'need' to close down the works. Once again private decisions were being taken in the Vickers Building in London which would have serious social consequences in the unemployment black spot of Tyneside. Once again trade unionists raised the questions – was closure unavoidable? Was the company right in maintaining there was no future for mechanical engineering on the Scotswood Road?

The workers decided to re-examine these issues from their own point of view, one which substituted a wider social efficiency for the narrow approach adopted by the company. Workers knew from their own experience that London had been running down the Tyneside plant for some time. As the *Workers' Enquiry into State Intervention* in industry put it,

> research and design was a low priority, the design team having been allowed to fall by nearly 90 per cent since 1960. Most of the products were made under licence from European or American companies, using their designs; investment had been low, machines and buildings were very old. For instance, some of the cranes were 60 years old, and many of the machines were pre-war.

This lack of attention to investment also led to the loss of potentially profitable orders. Not only was there a reluctance to develop new products or purchase new machinery but the company was even unwilling to spend money on maintenance. Again the workers' enquiry reports, 'there was only an understaffed central breakdown service. As a result, machines sometimes lay idle for several weeks.'

When workers opened the books at Scotswood they discovered what looked very much like a deliberate policy to close the plant down. The company seems to have been draining funds out of Scotswood with nothing going back to maintain it as an effective production unit. Management forecast that Scotswood would become heavily in debt to head office in the years ahead. In fact, management figures show that the Scotswood plant would have been expected to show a surplus by 1982 *in the absence of charges levied on the factory by Vickers' head office*. It is through the manipulation of such charges that managements can make profitable enterprises look extremely unprofitable should this be 'required' to further a company's overall objectives. Why would any private enterprise want to show a profitable plant to be making losses? The answer is simple: to give it more freedom to pursue higher profits elsewhere.

Of course, on an international scale, this is precisely what also goes on when export and import prices are deliberately chosen to shift profits around from country A to country B. Vickers workers performed an invaluable service in drawing attention to the need to challenge management's control over information as well as the decisions leading to job loss.

One of the many problems besetting the plant's activity was that its efforts were too thinly spread over a large number of different products. Among the goods the plant was traditionally renowned for were cranes, power presses and earth moving equipment. In order to compete successfully it was suggested by workers and their advisers that specialisation was required. This should have happened in the context of a comprehensive plan based on one or two products. The workers favoured power presses and, mindful of social need, recycling equipment. A substantial demand for these goods would have appeared within public sector nationalised industries and local authorities. Export possibilities also existed. What is more, the Labour government of the day could have taken the lead in putting this demand on a planned footing. However, substantial investment would be required to develop these products. If management's 'facts' were of such doubtful quality then surely workers could assess the viability of planned expenditures in an altogether more responsible fashion. Management's figures were taken as a starting point. Workers inquired into investment possibilities. All that was required was that a Labour government help to direct some public spending, in the form of purchasing, into Scotswood. There were clearly many kinds of benefits that could have been obtained in an alternative strategy for mechanical engineering on Tyneside. What was more, this was the only socially responsible strategy that existed. Scotswood workers went to great pains to point this out. Needless to say the social consequences of their actions mattered not one whit to management. There was simply no place in the balance sheet and appropriation account to enter social costs. The logic of private profitability does not recognise their existence.

What were the social costs of closure? First of all, lost jobs mean longer dole queues and an increase in the social security bill. Furthermore, the toll of lost jobs would go much further than the 750 or so skilled workers at Scotswood as the 'knock-on' effect resounded throughout the local community. Another 500 jobs could be expected to disappear for this reason. The total cost this could impose on local and central government could be expected to range from £3.2 million to £4.3 million, depending on the number of workers re-employed.

Second, there would be a cost to society in lost export markets and increased import penetration. Over a period of five years after closure it was anticipated that exports of between £10 million and £14 million would be lost. When these social costs are taken into account, there is absolutely no justification for the closure of Scotswood. It is also worthwhile noting that this conclusion stems from a fairly conservative calculation, one that takes no account of so-called intangible costs. These are the costs in personal hardship, wear and tear on social relationships in the family and elsewhere, demoralisation and ill-health following the loss of livelihood. The economics of common sense pointed unmistakably in one direction – preserve jobs and skills; avoid the waste and the huge social costs of unemployment, reject the private market logic of 'slimming for greater profitability'.

The Fairey Company and Tress Engineering

The Fairey corporation went bust in 1977. Workers in the Tress subsidiary on Tyneside were naturally concerned that jobs might be lost. This concern was, if anything, heightened when it seemed that the Trafalgar House group was developing an interest in some of the more profitable of Fairey's assets. Workers' anxiety was such that a vigorous campaign was mounted to persuade Labour's National Enterprise Board to take an interest in Fairey and in Tress. It was hoped that this would keep the asset-strippers at bay and lay the foundation for an assured future for production at Tress. The NEB did act, and, for a time, all seemed well. But a few months later, to the utter astonishment of the workforce, the NEB announced that due to Tress's lack of 'viability' it would have to close.

Abandoned by what they had thought was *their* government, workers once again began to build their own picture of what had been happening to Tress over the years. With a greater understanding of this, employees felt that they would be in a better position to defend their jobs. Once again it became clear, as in the Chrysler and Vickers case, that for years profits had been relentlessly sucked out of the Tress plant with nothing flowing in the opposite direction to maintain the plant's productive capacity. So long as this process continued, the Fairey managment had been reasonably happy. But when it seemed that Tress was about to move into the red, then business sense dictated one course of action – shut the plant down. Such was Fairey's interest in the future of Tress that, when in earlier years plant management had argued for greater investment funds, they were granted only at penal rates of interest. In fact the workers suggested that Fairey forced Tress to pay a higher rate of interest than a commercial bank would have demanded. Would it have been possible to avoid the waste and social cost associated with the closure of Tress?

Tress was a producer of valves for the petrochemical industry. Workers could see no reason why, with some investment in the plant and some diversification, the factory should not have a secure future. Even in Britain the oil industry was expanding rapidly and looked like doing so for some time ahead. Workers suggested that

> the government could use its various footholds in the economy to plan production and distribution . . . the government could now order valves for the oil refinery to be built near Aberdeen.

However, the government had no intention of embarking on any real planning exercise. It was more interested in assuring private business that firms 'assisted' by the NEB would receive no special help that might lead them to compete successfully with the private sector. There was no detailed calculation here of the social costs of closing Tress but there is no reason to believe that the answer found would have been unlike that at Vickers. Tress was a firm manufacturing a product with a demand that could easily have been secured by government intervention. A minimal amount of planning could have saved jobs. Instead the government turned its back on the workforce and let the NEB follow its market logic to the point of throwing another 300 workers onto the long dole queues of Tyneside.

Summary

As far as workers have been concerned the varied industrial encounters of the 1970s have been unpleasant. The end result was often redundancy. BL closed its Speke plant, Vickers closed down Scotswood, the NEB shut down Tress and even the well organised Lucas workers had redundancies forced upon them. As our list shows and as noted earlier, little distinguished the state from the purely private concern in the plant closure stakes. In the end the only difference seems to have been in the slightly slower rate at which the state boarded the doors and erected the For Sale or To Let signs. Socialist planning in the hands of the last Labour government amounted to no more than regulating the speed of redundancy.

Most of the stories told above are variations on one theme. Plants have been run down over a long period through lack of investment, as better opportunities for private profit have been exploited (often in poorly developed or authoritarian economies). As the health of Western economies has deteriorated in the 1970s, competition has grown fiercer and the weaknesses of British enterprise has become apparent. Managements typically reacted by announcing their intentions to cease such-and-such an operation in one spot, to relocate some other activity, and to shed labour.

In the above examples the workers responded in what would normally be described as a 'responsible' way by producing detailed and closely argued accounts of what had gone wrong and how the situation could be remedied while safeguarding jobs. Alternative strategies and workers' plans were developed and presented to management. The employers were not interested. In their view it was not for the workers to make decisions on how to run the plant. The workers turned to the Labour government for support. It was not interested. In its view the workers are there to vote in a general election, not to 'interfere' in the process of government. Individual plans like the Lucas workers' were well argued and convincing. The combine committee was even nominated on the strength of the plan for the 1979 Nobel peace prize. So why were Lucas workers not more successful in keeping jobs? The answer, surely, is that they were isolated. The government and the trade unions were not interested in encouraging workers throughout industry to take a plannng initiative. Because of the lack of a network of mutually supporting industry-wide workers' plans, those that we did see came to nothing.

All this was and is unfortunate but at least a number of lessons emerged through the experience. It showed that the basic planning problem was deeply rooted in the conflict between what was good for profits and what was good for working people. It also showed that there are alternatives to the logic of the market. Also there grew from the workplace a new practical economics which put social needs above profits.

5.

Local Planning to Save Jobs

Thatcherism can make your job disappear

After only one year in office Margaret Thatcher and her ministers had succeeded in doubling the number of people out of work. By the end of 1982 unemployment officially stood at almost 3.1 million. The true figure was much worse. The official statistics have never taken into account those who fail to register as unemployed or those who have only a temporary job provided by the state. In the autumn of 1982 the government became so desperate to show 'improvement' on jobs that it altered the basis of calculation of the unemployment statistics. Instead of a monthly count of those registering as unemployed at employment offices, the total now consists only of those receiving benefit. No matter how ingenious ministers may become in finding new justifications for including fewer and fewer of those out of work in the unemployment total, they cannot make the underlying upward trend disappear. December 1982 was the thirty-sixth month in a row to show an increase in unemployment.

It is clear that the Thatcher government has no interest in unemployment beyond ensuring that it is high enough to discipline workers. Ministers have even given up peddling the ridiculous idea that jobs can be found if enough energy is expended in the search. New depths of absurdity were plumbed by Norman Tebbit when he advised the unemployed to 'get on their bikes'. He and his colleagues seem now to recognise this.

In December 1979 for example, before things really deteriorated, six unemployed people chased every vacancy to appear. In December 1982 there were 26 people to every notified vacancy.

What is more, dispiriting though this average picture is, it fails to show how much more severely unemployment hits some groups than others – particularly the unskilled. If we went back to December 1979, when on average there were six unemployed to each vacancy, we would find that among 'general labourers' 50 people chased each job. In Wallsend on North Tyneside, in January 1981, 613 heavy labourers were registered as unemployed and two vacancies were notified to the Employment Office. Presumably Mr Tebbit's advice to the Wallsend unemployed would be to cycle, perhaps to North Shields, where a further four vacancies were reported to be available. Unfortunately, once there they would meet over 500 locally unemployed heavy labourers, even if a few of them had bikes and had gone in the opposite direction. It would do no good either to bike to West Moor or Whitley Bay since these had unemployed labourers but no vacancies at all.

Even London, in the relatively prosperous South East, at the end of 1982 had almost 400,000 without work. London's unemployed have trebled in number since Margaret Thatcher moved into Downing Street in May 1979. Over the river, above the County Hall, Ken Livingstone, the leader of the GLC, has erected a banner that records the capital's unemployment – a reminder to those in Westminster of the real cost of Thatcherism.

Can local authorities resist national policy?

It may seem that there is precious little that can be done by local authorities seeking to preserve jobs and reduce unemployment, given the restrictive economic policy pursued by central government. To be sure, so long as slump is the favoured policy in Whitehall, the scope for halting job attrition at the local level is limited. The towns and cities suffering greatest unemployment have few resources to throw into the battle for jobs. Government ministers make it their business to see that local authority finances are as tightly controlled as possible.

Despite this, in several places councillors have decided that some effort must be made to preserve jobs. The GLC has set up an Economic Policy Group (EPG) and the Greater London Enterprise Board (GLEB); the West Midlands County Council has established its own West Midlands Enterprise Board (WMEB); Sheffield has its Employment Committee; Fife is interested in the

West Midlands experiment. Throughout the country many local authorities are desperately searching for some defence against Thatcherism.

There is a strong thread of continuity between the various workers' struggles of the 1970s, mentioned in the previous chapter, and recent local authority economic initiatives. Many of those people who were actively involved in the purely industrial events of the 1970s are now helping to shape local strategies to defend jobs. Mike Cooley, for example, a leading figure behind the Lucas Plan, became one of the first members of the GLC's Economic Policy Group. Hilary Wainwright, who had been involved in workers' campaigns for jobs on Tyneside as well as with the Lucas Plan in the 1970s, also became a member of the London Economic Policy Group. The team is headed by Robin Murray, who was previously best known for his work on economic development and multinationals. In Sheffield, John Bennington, formerly of Coventry Workshop (a trade union and community research centre), is Chief Employment Officer. Coventry Workshop had been particularly active in the struggle of motor and machine tool industry workers as they fought to hang on to their jobs in the 1970s. Geoffrey Edge was a minister in the last Labour government and now chairs the West Midlands Enterprise Board and the council's Economic Development Committee. Current local authority initiatives also involve others whose experience may be useful in defending jobs. Richard Minns has spent much time investigating the deficiencies of British investment institutions, notably the pension funds, and now works for the West Midlands Enterprise Board. But even with such impressive personnel, what can local authorities realistically hope to achieve? How many jobs will they be able to save? How, precisely, will socialists in capitalist Britain act, to defend labour and maintain employment?

Socialist policy for London

As in almost every other part of the country, the growth in unemployment has accelerated in London since Margaret Thatcher became prime minister. In May 1979, 130,000 Londoners were out of work. In late 1982 the figure was close to 400,000. What can a single socialist local authority do to stem the flood of jobs being lost?

To start with, it is important to understand what is happening to the London economy. While Thatcherism has been a disaster for London, a look at the figures shows that even before 1979 all was not well. The British economy began to see its manufacturing sector wasting away in the 1970s. London did not escape from this process. Between 1971 and 1981 the capital lost 400,000 manufacturing jobs. This 'de-industrialisation', or decline of the industrial economy, of London in the 1970s was only a more dramatic phase in a process which began in the late fifties. In 1951 London had around 1.5 million manufacturing jobs: in 1982 barely 550,000 remained. Manufacturing accounted for 36 per cent of London's total employment in 1951. It has been estimated that by 1985 this share will have been reduced to 17 per cent.

The British economy has been losing manufacturing jobs for a long time. The same is true of London. British firms, unable to compete in world markets, have either been 'disciplined' out of existence or have restructured their operations, often relocating manufacturing to countries where labour is cheaper and less well organised. On a national level Thatcherism can be viewed as an economic policy designed to speed up this process. Is there anything that a single local authority can do to resist international economic pressures, pressures which in the UK are reinforced by the Tory government?

The Labour-controlled GLC is convinced that something can be done. Under existing legislation the GLC is able to raise a relatively small amount of money on the rates for special purposes so long as it is spent in the 'interests of all or some of the people of London'. This source will yield around £40 million each year and will provide the basic budget to support London's economic initiatives to save jobs. It is of course grossly inadequate given the 400,000 already unemployed. There will be no about-turn in the capital's economic fortunes because the GLC spends £40 million or so every year on job support schemes. In purely job terms all that can be hoped for, in the *Financial Times*'s estimation, is that by 1985 perhaps 10,000 jobs may have been saved or created.

The GLC expects realistically modest results from its economic policy. With more resources, more jobs could be saved. If central government embraced a job-creating instead of job-destroying economic policy, even more would be achieved. None the less the GLC's economic intervention has an importance which goes beyond any attempt to measure immediate success in numbers of jobs. It lies in the fact that a local authority is trying to understand the process of capitalist restructuring, which is laying waste its economy, *and* looking for ways to intervene to influence the restructuring process *in the interests of labour*. The basic assumption of the Economic Policy Group is that it is possible for local authorities to have an impact on reshaping, for the benefit of ordinary people, what previously was considered to be purely private capitalist decision-making.

This highly interventionist approach to local economic policy is also important because it breaks with the tradition of trying to tempt firms into a particular area with lavish incentive packages. The 1970s witnessed a fierce and almost totally counter-productive competition between local authorities to capture supposedly 'footloose' capital. From East Kilbride to Peterborough, from the highlands of Scotland to the valleys of Wales, the development agencies have competed with each other to provide factory units, to knock a percentage point off interest rates, to add a year to the rent-free holiday, and so on. In the late 1970s it became fashionable to see small and new firms as the seedcorn of economic regeneration. Local authorities set up small firms advisory bureaux and enterprise boards to try to release the animal spirit of the entrepreneur in their areas. The results of these policies were rarely impressive and the GLC in the early 1980s has firmly rejected them.

The GLC does not see itself as an agency that preserves employment simply by subsidising private firms. If it were merely a matter of subsidy then the more money spent the more would be the jobs created, but then as soon as the money ran out so too would the jobs disappear. The Economic Policy Group well understands that lasting job creation will only be a reality in the present world if competitiveness can be secured. The point is that there is not just one route to competitiveness, the way of the long dole queue.

Technology, for example, need not develop in the way it does under capitalism, destroying skills, dehumanising labour, making jobs vanish. There is no reason why new technologies should not be job- and skill-generating. Members of the EPG strongly believe that the direction of technological development can be influenced, that it can be pushed towards benefiting people rather than throwing them out of work.

We will have to wait a while before the success of these initiatives can properly be judged. In the meantime the GLC has on its side a strong argument built simply on the evident waste of capitalism. The stock of readily available skills among London's 400,000 unemployed must be enormous. The jobs that need doing – the social needs of the capital – are known to be huge. It should be a simple matter to make great improvements to the quality of life in London by matching the two. The private decision-making which is so dominant in capitalism has nothing to contribute. The EPG intends to fill the gap by devising ways of bringing wasted assets into socially useful production.

To work properly there has to be a basic flow of ideas coming from workers and community groups. Of course these are unlikely to appear on any great scale spontaneously and because of this the Economic Policy Group is concerned to take steps to stimulate them. It has an educational programme designed to explain to Londoners how it can be approached to provide the resources required to develop economic ideas. A forum has been set up, the Popular Planning Assembly, to which trade union, community and other groups can send delegates, and whose main aim will be the encouragement of wider discussion on how to save jobs and make use of London's wasted resources. From this, it is hoped, will come ideas that will contribute to the construction of a London industrial strategy. The existence of such a strong participative element in economic policy reflects the awareness of many of those in the Economic Policy Group of the failure of the last Labour government to involve people in its ill-fated industrial strategy. Developing an industrial and labourpower plan for London is, according to Ken Livingstone, 'to be an exercise in democratic planning . . . with the active involvement of trade union and community groups on a wide scale'.

The EPG has found itself operating on two fronts. As soon as it was set up in the summer of 1982, workers threatened with redundancy came to it for help. At the same time the EPG has been devising its own broad intentions for economic action.

Some working principles had to be quickly established for dealing with workers whose firms were in difficulty. First, could management decisions be reversed? Were particular union branches strong enough to challenge management? In some cases, the council's economic intervention might just help to tip the balance in favour of economic decisions more in the workers' interests. In others, managements's decisions might have to be accepted. But even in those cases, the EPG could encourage the movement to a second line of defence; could some sort of alternative strategy be developed which workers might successfully pursue independently of management? Could something at least be salvaged from the wreckage left behind in the reckless pursuit of private profits?

While immediate positions were being worked out for dealing with crisis situations, longer-term ideas were also being developed. The need for a London industrial strategy was obvious. This had to be produced in a democratic manner, one that would involve as many people as possible. Further, as an instrument of economic intervention, the Greater London Enterprise Board was set up.

The GLEB is quite unlike any enterprise board, national or local, of the 1970s. Alan McGarvey, its chief executive, explains that the purpose of the GLEB is, 'to play an active role in economic development, involving the preparation of strategies and taking the lead on major investment projects'. There is nothing unusual in that, nor in the fact that 'it is our intention to invest in the creation of new and expanding firms, as well as offering assistance to firms which are basically viable but in temporary difficulty'. But its style of operating will be quite different from, say, that of the National Enterprise Board. The reason is that, in McGarvey's words:

> we will seek, wherever possible, to involve ordinary people who can discuss their needs as consumers, as residents or workers and can play a part in the industrial restructuring of their environment.

The GLEB is also different from previous local enterprise boards in being oriented towards medium-to-large firms rather than the small firms which local authorities focused on in the past. In practical terms the GLEB is the conduit through which money raised through the rates is channelled, in pursuit of the London industrial strategy 'in the interests of all or some of the people of London'.

In their first few months of devising new economic policies for London, members of the EPG have made some headway but also suffered some disappointment. The loss to London of Staffa Engineering was probably the first disappointment. Its parent holding company was intent on relocating the Staffa activity from the East

End of London to Plymouth, partly in order to take advantage of a government development grant. The workers put up a fight locally but elsewhere in the combine, as well as in the relevant trade union (the AUEW), the determination to resist the move was lacking. In these circumstances, the GLC could do little. Most jobs were lost. Nevertheless, a couple of projects have been initiated which may salvage thirty or so jobs from the wreckage.

Fortunately, three more hopeful examples of council intervention in defence of workers exist. Lee Cooper, like Staffa, wanted rationalisation. As part of the restructuring process it decided to close its Romford factory with the loss of 200 jobs. Lack of any organisation in the factory made it impossible to challenge management's decision. The Economic Policy Group contributed advice and a grant to explore the possibilities of forming a co-operative.

This resulted in 12 women from Lee Cooper deciding to go ahead and start manufacturing children's clothes, with regular consultations with families on an enormous council estate nearby. Clothes would be designed with the active involvement of people on the estate. The GLC's intervention meant that skills which would otherwise have been wasted could be put to use in satisfying real social and local needs. What is more, the style of intervention was one that for the first time brought different groups of people together in solving common problems. The skilled women's need for work was brought alongside the need of families for good quality and inexpensive clothing for their children. The GLEB did not exist at the time but Alan McGarvey would have approved the venture as exactly in line with the board's philosophy that

> it should provide the mechanism whereby all those with a direct interest in developing new sources of employment are able to get together to stimulate new business.

Associated Automation was a subsidiary of GEC, manufacturing telephone coin box equipment in Willesden. It was a line of business which, though profitable, was not profitable enough for GEC. In earlier years the workers had successfully resisted the company's attempts to close the plant, but in 1982 management could afford to sit out any strike. With the aid of the GLC the workers explored the possibility of a 'buy-out', deciding in the end that they could survive as a going concern independently of GEC. Existing products would ensure the new co-operative's immediate future, but long-term viability would be dependent on new product development. Thanks to the GLC's intervention, 182 jobs were saved, but whether this is a lasting gain remains to be seen.

Many, but not all of London's economic problems stem from large firms reorganising themselves. A large number of companies are simply going bust. Such was the case at Austinsuite Furniture in Leyton. Here, a local medium-sized firm with about 400 employees had serious trading problems and a large overdraft with Barclays. The bank was committed to the tune of some £1.8 million and decided to cut its losses. The Economic Policy Group wanted to intervene and try to save some jobs in a particularly depressed part of London. Luckily a new buyer was found for the company and with financial support from the GLC, and at least the acquiescence of the bank, furniture production continues in London's East End.

To show that there is a credible socialist alternative to the waste of capitalist restructuring, more will have to be done by the GLC than engaging in what are basically rescue operations to defend jobs. Where the GLC has intervened in support of workers, it has done so to avoid the sheer waste of unemployment. A socialist economic strategy obviously must show that it can avoid that waste if it is to stand any chance of being persuasive. Preventing future unemployment is one thing but it is also necessary to show that much can be done with the resources *already* consigned to the dustbin by policies guided only by profits.

The most basic principle accepted by the Economic Policy Group is that currently wasted resources *can* be brought into good use to meet some of the pressing needs of Londoners. If capitalism cannot provide a form of economic organisation capable of this, then it is worthwhile thinking about how it might be done. It is also a basic belief of the EPG that the thinking needs to be done by the people most affected. This leads to a style of intervention where the GLC will provide the resources to encourage people to take economic and social problems into their own hands. There will be no grand plan for the economic recovery of London designed by experts in the County Hall and laid before the masses like a set of commandments. It is hoped that there will be a plan, the London economic strategy mentioned earlier, but as Ken Livingstone has said, it will be devised through the widest possible discussion.

What has happened so far in making a reality of the idea that waste can be avoided? Two campaigns have been launched to bring unused resources together with unmet social needs, and both are rapidly gaining momentum. They are becoming better known as 'Jobs from Warmth' and 'Jobs from Childcare'.

'Jobs from Warmth'

Council tenants know only too well the economics of energy. It is often simply too expensive. In London in 1982, 32,000 people had their electricity supply cut off, mostly because they could not afford to pay their bills. On the post-war Harvest estate in Islington, bills of around £300 a quarter have not been unusual. On another Islington estate, the Delhi-Outram estate, annual heating costs to tenants average £500 to £700. This estate is supposed to benefit from alleged economies in heat supplied on a district-wide basis. In those council flats where people have some control over their own heating, they choose simply to switch it off, preferring the cold to the anxiety caused by the final reminders.

Tenants are rightly unhappy that they have so little control over heating systems for their own homes. Private householders faced with similar problems of inefficient and expensive heating would soon act to change their systems. Home-improvement loans would be obtained (with tax relief on interest payments) and insulation would be put in, perhaps also a gas rather than an oil or electric boiler.

The stimulus to a more sensible approach to local heating problems in London came from a group of trade unionists, community workers and tenants in Islington. Discussions about the problem have taken place between residents and workers. The Islington 'Jobs from Warmth' Group was set up to carry the campaign forward. The GLC could do two things. First, it could provide funds through the GLEB, if it seemed that some proposals might emerge which a bit of 'pump-priming' would get off the ground. One idea is to produce appropriate heating equipment in a municipal factory. Some useful technical work on cheap heating devices had been carried out by Lucas workers. The result was a heat pump working on the principle of a refrigerator in reverse. It would not generate energy but it would convert cold into hot air up to three times more efficiently than if fuel was burnt conventionally. This sort of equipment, for which there must be a huge, if latent, local authority market, is just the kind of socially useful product that the GLEB is interested in.

The second thing the GLC could do and has done is to provide technical advice and assistance to tenants and workers. The Economic Policy Group provides this help through a 'technology network'. The London energy and employment network, initially based at County Hall, will move out to three separate centres in London. Accommodation will be provided by the Polytechnic of Central London and the Polytechnic of the South Bank. Further technology networks are planned for other product areas. Their purpose, as Hilary Wainwright explains in *Capital and Class*, is to

> harness the grossly underused facilities of London's polytechnics and universities, for the use of trade unionists and others who wish to develop employment plans either as bargaining positions in the company they work for or as the basis of a co-operative or municipal enterprise. The networks will for instance develop a 'product bank' of prototypes of new products of a socially useful kind that would be available for such groups.

In Islington, as elsewhere, many people with skills relevant to these technical problems are unemployed. Their skills are being wasted. If ways can be found of putting them to work then in a real sense Islington, London and the country as a whole would be getting something for nothing. It is costly to keep people unemployed. Above and beyond the money a humane and civilised society must spend on supporting the unemployed and their families, there is the enormous cost to society of the output that is lost through unemployment. Then, in the energy field, there is a crucial question of efficiency. Many post-war housing estates are equipped with just the opposite of efficient heating systems. We are constantly told that we are approaching, if not already living in, an age of energy shortage. It is quite clear what sensible decision-makers would do given this; they would encourage greater efficiency in the way we use energy.

The easy answer to this would be (and has been) to put the price of energy up; but it is plain that this alone is not a socially responsible attitude. Large resource savings could quickly and easily be made through using untapped, unemployed skills to meet real social needs. Putting resources into more efficient energy use would also reduce the need for enormously expensive investment in new generating plant. It is estimated that it costs 3 to 10 times more to supply a watt of energy by building new plant than to save a watt through energy conservation such as building insulation. Despite this, the Central Electricity Generating Board is committed to building expensive and potentially lethal water-cooled nuclear reactors bought from the United States in a national programme worth up to £20 billion.

'Jobs from Childcare'

The right to work applies as much to women as it does to men. But women will not be able to take up fulfilling work outside the home so long as the extent of domestic labour is unrecognised and so unevenly shared. The view of the Economic Policy Group is that jobs can be created by organising childcare in new and collective ways. Indeed, it is absolutely essential to the participative element in drawing up a plan for London's economy that women have the opportunity to get involved. Earlier, Ken Livingstone's description of democratic planning as one involving the widest possible number of people was quoted. In fact, he went on to say, almost in the same breath:

> Every effort will be made to encourage and provide the necessary resources for women – both in the home and in employment – to contribute their ideas and their needs to the planning process.

Many ideas for childcare projects exist throughout London and many local groups are working on them. The GLC may be able to provide initial funding to launch a number of childcare centres where working parents can leave children, where they will be fed, and where there will be laundry facilities. Where a firm's workers benefited from this, the firm would be expected to contribute towards funding.

The needs of families and children for clothes, for toys, for educational material (especially good books), can be met by matching unemployed skills to unmet needs in London. The role of the EPG or, if appropriate, the GLEB is to facilitate the match, to help provide the organisational framework to sustain, in this case, jobs from childcare.

An experiment along these lines is actually underway in Lambeth, where Asian women have formed a co-operative to make toys. Useful employment is provided, serving the important need of children for toys and books with different ethnic images. The idea itself came from discussions between mothers, nursery workers and teachers. The work is skilled, and training is given in, for example, carpentry. A nursery is available with workers to look after the children, giving members of the co-operative a new freedom to develop skills and to participate in rewarding work outside the home.

Socialist policy for the West Midlands

The recession has been felt particularly severely in the West Midlands. At the end of 1982, with unemployment at a national average of over 13 per cent, in the West Midlands the average was 17 per cent. In some inner city areas, almost one worker in three was without work. While the government persisted with its slump policies, the local authority felt that it should try to find some means of halting the downward slide.

The council's Economic Development Committee proposed a strategy for the area in a document published in November 1981. It suggested that policy should have two strands: an industrial strategy for the region and a distinct community strategy. The former would concern itself with 'reviving investment and employment in the West Midlands industry', the latter would be designed to

> improve training, increase the take-up of welfare benefits, attack 'illegal' low pay, provide work opportunities and counselling for the unemployed, assist local voluntary groups and so on.

As in London, an enterprise board, the WMEB, would be set up to act as principal agent in furthering the *industrial* strategy. Again, as in London, initial funding would come from the rates, giving the Board a budget of around £3.5 million. The WMEB would be concerned with using this money to produce jobs that would stand the test of competitiveness.

However, behind some striking similarities, important differences exist between Greater London and West Midlands Enterprise Boards. The role of the WMEB is more sharply defined as an instrument of industrial policy. Wider social considerations are taken into account, not by the Board but by the council in its Economic Development Committee. Geoff Edge, the Board's chair, makes this clear: 'We take a commerical view of the projects. If a company is not viable in the long term then we do not want to know.' (*Financial Times*, 18 August 1982).

It is confirmed by Richard Minns, who explains that 'WMEB itself does not do any social cost-benefit analysis. The county council will identify the wider benefits of the Board's activity.' In London on the other hand, while the GLEB is also committed, according to its chief executive, 'to support only projects which are efficiently run and have good prospects of viability' it is clear that the accounting, prior to decisions being taken, will be done in a substantially different way. The GLEB, as Alan McGarvey clearly puts it,

> will take into account the cost of unemployment, the cost of lost skills, and the cost of wasted land. It will recognise the special benefits of increased investment in the areas of high unemployment. It will consider how far a project gives working people more control over economic decisions. And it will assess the possible benefits of a project, from the point of view of women and ethnic minorities.

Both Enterprise Boards want to create stable long-run employment opportunities, but it is clear that each has a different idea of the kind of accounting that is appropriate to making the best decisions. In particular, subsidy is explicitly ruled out in the West Midlands case, but not it seems in London. Alan McGarvey is quite clear that his Board 'is not in the business of producing jobs for only a few weeks or months', but Hilary Wainwright is equally certain that

> the GLC intends to innovate and reorganise in a way which will be of benefit to labour, without necessarily being profitable in the case of each and every project.

This at least allows the possibility of subsidy. There is nothing harmful in this of course, so long as enough profitable projects are generated to carry the others. Where difficulties may emerge in London, but not for the WMEB, is in selecting projects. This is simply because London's social criteria, not excluding subsidy, are bound to generate many more possibilities.

The basic assumption of the WMEB, which serves also to justify its existence, is that many firms are in danger of being lost because of essentially short-term cash-flow problems. That is, if financial institutions (banks, pension funds and so on) would only help such firms to restructure their finances rather than pull out when difficulties threaten, then the long-term future of many firms might be secured. If those institutions were prepared to take equity in firms and otherwise provide long-term finance, then many more firms might survive the recession.

The WMEB sees its role as helping firms to put their finances on a sound footing. Stuart Burchall, another WMEB member, describes the Board as, 'a novel financial institution with objectives very different from those of existing financial institutions'. It will give loans (at commercial rates of interest), but it prefers to take shares – an equity stake – in companies. It believes that the private capital market has so far failed to give firms the kind of financial assistance they need and, in the end, could pay for. Crucially, it also believes that it can persuade financial institutions, and in particular the pension funds, to go in with it. Indeed without that happening, the £3.5 million it has to spend would have barely perceptible effects on the West Midlands economy.

The economic initiatives of the West Midlands Council are, like those of the Greater London Council, aimed at intervening in the economy on the side of labour. Creating long-term jobs is the main objective. Geoff Edge claims that the WMEB will soon be well on the way to its target of saving or creating 5,000 jobs each year. Apart from the long-run return the WMEB expects on its investments, it also promotes a 'good employer regime' and insists on the production of a 'planning and investment agreement' between itself and the firm concerned. So far, trade-union assistance in shaping planning agreements has been modest. None the less the agreements are important to the council, and firms that refuse to participate in them are quickly sent on their way. Generally speaking the popular participation that is emphasised in London's economic policy is replaced in the West Midlands by emphasis on the need to secure pension fund participation in investment for long-term jobs.

By December 1982 the WMEB had made six investments. It had committed almost £1.9 million, but had successfuly prised from the financial institutions £3.70 for every £1 it spent. A total of 785 jobs were secured. On average each job cost the council £2,382, a small sum compared to the cost of supporting unemployment and consequent losses in output. The Enterprise Board also believes that it will make a good return on these investments, a belief that is given some weight by private sector participation.

Four of the firms supported by local authority action are foundries. The first company to be saved from collapse was Sage Aluminium Products of Wolverhampton, a producer of high pressure castings more than 30 per cent of which go to Ford. The firm has good market prospects and WMEB intervention helped to restructure its finances. Dudley Foundry Ltd had gone into receivership but was only one of three firms in the country making heavy S-iron castings. Financial support was given to a new venture partly on the grounds of the special nature of the product and the difficulty customers would have in finding alternative supplies. Armalloy was another foundry, supported this time on the grounds of good export potential. Butler Foundry Ltd was a firm that had taken advantage of government aid in the 1970s for modernisation, but having had to complete the process itself, became crippled by huge interest repayments. The WMEB intervened to help the company restructure its balance sheet, provided it with long-term capital and saved 120 jobs. In another instructive case the WMEB financed a management 'buy-out' which could actually have gone ahead with funds from an alternative source. The Enterprise Board's offer to take an equity stake in the firm gave the company room for manoeuvre and freedom from the large interest payments on the other loan offered. The remaining investment was in the form of money to finance exports and was seen as a 'one-off', not typical of the equity role desired by the West Midlands Enterprise Board.

As part of its broader strategy for jobs, West Midlands County Council is also involved in a number of initiatives with parallels in London. The council will, through its Economic Development Unit, go on the offensive with workers who are struggling to put forward their own alternatives to redundancy. When it seemed that BL workers at Guys Motors in Wolverhampton might set up a co-operative in response to management's closure plans, the Economic Development Unit offered assistance. The council is also interested in alternative products and has funded a unit at Coventry Polytechnic to investigate possibilities.

There is no doubt however that the emphasis of West Midlands jobs strategy differs from that of London. The WMEB is trying to find a niche for itself among financial institutions. It has spotted what it believes is a 'gap' in the capital market (the unwillingness of the institutions to place long-term funds in manufacturing), and it hopes that by moving towards that gap it will take some of the resources of the pension funds with it. At the time of writing the WMEB is trying to set up a new account to which it will contribute

£3 million and to which it hopes up to six other institutions can be tempted to invest £500,000 each. The WMEB will then use the £6 million fund for investment in around 12 West Midlands companies. In London, on the other hand, the policy emphasises demonstrating, with real examples, how to use wasted resources to satisfy social need.

How much is likely to be achieved?

In the West Midlands some 785 workers had benefited through the activity of the local enterprise board by the end of 1982. It is hoped that the complete package of policies, of which the Board is one part only, might be able to save 5,000 jobs each year. Compared to the hundreds of thousands out of work in the region, these numbers have little meaning. In the West Midlands they are aware, only too aware, of the limitations on their efforts against unemployment. As Geoff Edge has put it, 'There is no way the Enterprise Board on its own can reflate the economy.'

In London, economic policy has been less constrained, in the sense that there is no overriding focus on the deficiencies of financial institutions. Economic initiatives have been more wide-ranging and so, at least to start with, more exciting but (in early 1983) with modest results. Of the 200 or so workers who were employed by Lee Cooper only 12 arrived in the new co-operative to produce children's clothes. Austinsuite had employed 400 before receivership; the GLC deal saved 150 jobs. The GEC subsidiary, Associated Automation, employed about 350 when its closure was announced; the intervention of the GLC meant that around 180 jobs were saved. Altogether then from these and two other projects the GLC can be credited with around 600 jobs. We know that the Economic Policy Group has ideas going far beyond bailing out weak firms – to making use of currently wasted resources and matching unemployed skills with social needs. But the EPG is also realistic about what is possible. As it explains: 'One local authority such as the GLC cannot solve problems which have national and international repercussions.'

So what can be achieved by one socialist local authority like the GLC? The answer is – demonstration. Each small project that gets off the ground, which brings together unemployed resources in socially useful production, shows that there is a socialist economics of common sense. Every example of this sort gives the lie to Thatcherism and its doctrine that unemployment is inevitable.

In the West Midlands they also hope they are demonstrating the possibilities of a socialist economic strategy. There the immediate target is not 'Jobs from Warmth' or 'Jobs from Childcare' but the huge resources of the pension funds. The aim is to persuade the pension funds that they are not at present serving their members' interests well by investing in property (such as shopping centres) or in company shares on the stock exchange. Instead, the real rate of return on their investments (which are, incidentally, financed by the savings of millions of workers in company and trade union pension schemes) would be greater if a longer-term view were taken and more funds placed in British manufacturing.

It is a hard argument to win. The professional management of the pension funds and their City advisers are likely to be against such a radical shift in investment strategy. However the view in the West Midlands is that local authorities, together with trade union trustees of pension funds, can stimulate the demand for greater accountability in the way these savings are invested. The hope is that the narrow criterion of short-term profitability can be successfully challenged. As Richard Minns has put it in his *Take over the City*,

> the interests of people as workers and savers can only be improved by social and democratic control over finance as part of an alternative strategy for investment and growth.

It is in demonstrating this alternative that the West Midlands Enterprise Board sees a role for itself.

The existence of interventionist policies in the defence of jobs depends of course on the willingness of local authorities to take suitable action. This in turn depends on their political complexion and confers an air of transience on such policies. Would anything be left of local economic initiative if the Labour Party lost control of these areas?

In each case the answer is likely to be yes, though for rather different reasons. In the West Midlands the activity of the local enterprise board probably commands a bipartisan political support because even Tory councillors are likely by now to be less sanguine about national policies which have such devastating local effect. It would come as no surprise if the West Midlands Confederation of British Industry also tacitly supported the council's economic initiative. If private capital were persuaded that the local authority was simply correcting a failure of the market mechanism then it too might find the enterprise board acceptable. Given this, the WMEB might carve for itself a permanent place among instruments of council policy.

The same cannot be said for the economic *policies* of the Labour GLC. Popular planning for social need will be seen as a threat by many business people. To win their support the Economic Policy Group would have to embrace narrower and more sharply defined economic policies. It would need to persuade the business community, and local Tories, that there were strict self-imposed limits on the scope of the council's economic interventions. Instead, the GLC will try to demonstrate, for the first time in post-war Britain, that it is possible to bring wasted assets into the production of socially useful products. The council has prepared guidelines for defining 'socially useful':

> in manufacture and in use it conserves energy and materials; and its manufacture, repairs, and the recycling of its products can be carried out by non-alienating labour; and that its production and its products should assist human beings rather than maiming them.

It has defined criteria for investment selection which, in most board rooms of British industry, would be as incomprehensible as if they had been written in Chinese. Hilary Wainwright again explains:

> A social basis for investment appraisal has been drawn up providing for higher financial support according to whether the enterprise is based on some form of social ownership and control, how many employees are blacks or women, how many apprenticeships are created, how high are the wages paid, and how long the jobs are maintained.

There can be little doubt that if Labour lost its hold on County Hall all this would change. Most probably the Tories would once more set up small firm advice centres and send emissaries to New York to try to lure American capital to London. Nevertheless confidence would survive, a confidence among at least some workers and tenants, that it is possible to act, to do something about inadequate expensive heating or the lack of childcare facilities, to do something about the fact that needs like these could be met from the great pool of unemployment in London.

The structure of popular planning could also survive unwelcome political change in the capital. Members of the Economic Policy Group see their job as providing encouragement to workplace and community groups so that they can develop their own solutions to the problems they face. A network of community and trade union research centres is being set up to provide the back-up needed by people. The technology networks based on the five London Polytechnics are also located outside the GLC and serve the same purpose. If popular planning is to succeed then it has to have a strong base outside County Hall and to be in a sense independent of the GLC. The council can begin to provide funds to get things moving and Hilary Wainwright hopes that 'these resources will help strengthen workers' organisations in a way which cannot be reversed by a change in political control of the GLC'. The educational programme that the council plans to mount to explain and win people over to its policies is a crucial part of any socialist strategy for jobs in London. Through it, people themselves will see how the council can support them in taking economic and social problems into their own hands. We will see develop in London examples of a new approach to economics – a common sense economics which starts not from profits but from unused resources and unmet needs. This spelling out of socialist principles and the attempt to apply them – especially in a hostile environment – can have immense political and educational significance even if their immediate results in actual jobs created or saved in 1983 or 1984 are limited.

6.

The Economics of Common Sense

Over recent years the supposed wisdom of free market economics has been condensed into a number of themes against which argument appears difficult. The most popular of these is that, as individuals, we regularly 'pay ourselves more than we earn' and, on a national level, government has ignored the basic principles of 'sound finance' by borrowing without restraint. It is alleged that we lived foolishly during the 1950s and 1960s on borrowed money and borrowed time. The argument continues that we are now paying the inevitable price for past profligacy: 4 million unemployed. Neither has this been a purely Tory argument. An important contribution to the development of this (market) logic was made by previous Labour governments, whose policies may be neatly summed up in James Callaghan's dictum that 'we cannot spend our way out of a recession'.

The result is a UK recession in which the pay packet is disciplined by the simple threat of unemployment. Of course the policy has all sorts of contradictory effects and some businesses find that they too may get 'disciplined' out of the market place. By and large, though, big business supports this method of educating labour about the 'laws of the market'.

It should be clear however that this business common sense is very limited. There is nothing in it except unemployment and low wages for working people. There is no reason why workers should accept it. But so long as alternatives seem fanciful, its appeal may be understandable. What we need is an economics of common sense which workers can easily identify with and see to be in their interest. Only a system of socialist planning can offer this. The principles of such a system clearly exist, and the industrial experience of the 1970s as well as the regional experience of the early eighties begin to show that planning is also an intensely practical affair.

First, all economic activity should be directed to the satisfaction of social needs. Second, social needs can only be identified, and priorities established, on the basis of developing socially responsible forms of decision-making: democracy must be enriched. Third, unemployment is wasteful, and reasonable men and women would not permit it to exist. Fourth, in an attempt to become a competitive manufacturer in international terms, unemployed resources put to work give us something for nothing.

These principles contrast sharply with the logic of the market. In capitalist economies, private profit at any social cost is the force that drives the system. Decisions are also made privately and subject to no effective scrutiny as to social consequences. In this sense the system lacks a democracy which the five-yearly dusting down of ballot boxes helps to conceal. Unemployment, in this system, is perfectly tolerable even at high levels and for long periods. Under present arrangements, competitiveness is best fostered by throwing people out of work.

New technologies may be developed to promote competitiveness, but lack of social accountability will ensure that this happens to the detriment of working people.

Social need

First of all, as noted earlier, Labour's planning proposals do not satisfactorily stress the importance of social need. This has bred the suspicion in the minds of some trade unionists that a future Labour government may lose its sense of direction. This happened in the 1970s and it may happen again. Such anxiety has led several trades councils to produce a statement of what socialist planning should seek to achieve. In *Popular Planning for Social Need*, they declare:

> We believe that an effective alternative strategy from a trade union point of view has to reject competitive success as the object of industrial reconstruction.

Yet it is undeniable that competitiveness *is* an important goal, at least in the short term, the international capitalist market being what it is. The crucial question is, who should control the process of becoming competitive? Labour Party documents say workers should have this power, but many people are not convinced that the party has its heart in this. What would help here would be an alternative social strategy which would clearly show that Labour's economics is an *economics of social need*. For this the party must have objectives in its new planning proposals which are unambiguously 'social' in nature and which will have at least the same rank as that currently commanded by competitiveness in labour-movement discussion. An alternative social and economic strategy is needed which will demonstrate, in the words of the trades councils above, 'that we stand for a just and humane society'.

Democracy

Only popular discussion can decide on the particular social objectives that government should embrace. It could be to look for some measurable improvement in the health or housing of working people, as well as to reduce unemployment to below one million. On the other hand perhaps we should start from a completely different question like the one suggested by Anna Coote in a *New Socialist* article, 'How shall we care for and support our children?'.

The answer to the question, 'what kind of social strategy?', can only be found in society-wide debate, so much more support is likely to be generated for it than exists at present for the alternative economic strategy (AES). We would then have an alternative social *and* economic strategy which would be the property of the many people who produced it and would offer a much more convincing alternative to Thatcherism.

We also need to begin to prepare even now a more detailed planning in the workplace and in the local community. The trade unions could start the ball rolling by developing alternative plans for firms and sectors with jobs particularly at risk. Wherever private decision-making is likely to produce social damage, it should be called to account. The experience of the 1970s shows us that management's logic *can* be challenged, that counter-strategies *can* be devised. Of course the weight of an alternative plan is unlikely to be enough on its own to win a fight for jobs in the current climate, but every challenge to private decision-making advertises the real alternative ways of doing things.

The style of Labour Party policy-making has improved over recent years. It is much more open today. The continuing dicussion on the AES stands as testimony to this. However there is a current of thought in the party that simply cannot consider planning except in the most abstract and technical terms. Jeremy Bray, a Labour MP, is perhaps the chief exponent of this technocratic planning. Large corporations would supply the government with computer programs, or models, representing the way they behave. Devising socialist economic policy would become a computer problem-solving exercise. The socialist plan would be read off a television screen or, more probably, a visual display unit. As Bray has recently, but none too clearly, put it in the *New Statesman*:

> To take advantage of available technology and to minimise bureaucracy, companies could be required to mount their models in standard software on a particular make of micro-computer and left connected to a telephone line overnight, so that an automatic multiplexer connected to the Treasury model, by ringing up and exchanging passwords, could obtain any required solutions.

Whatever this means, we can see that Bray's socialist planning, based on micro-computers, automatic multiplexers and computer passwords, is strictly for those in the know. It would be unfortunate if this ever became the dominant view of planning in the Labour Party. One of its main weaknesses is that it is purged of social content. It is a picture of planning in a social vacuum where there are no classes with opposing interests. It hardly mentions working people and certainly requires no more from them than predictable behaviour. Whatever else it may be, it is not socialist planning as we understand it. But it does forcibly point to the need for democracy in planning. It also shows us that there is a huge need for knowledge itself to be democratised.

Labour has proposed to set up a new planning college in its recent policy statements. It is a nice idea – provided it can avoid becoming an elitist institution. But it is not what people need most to help them challenge capitalist decision-making. Much more useful would be a party commitment to extend the existing but inadequate network of trade union and community research centres. Every town should have its centre – partly socialist advice bureau, partly forum to exchange planning ideas. These could be immensely helpful in providing the back-up to workers who need to challenge their bosses' plans for the workplace. Some local authorities, as we have seen, are experimenting with new forms of local enterprise to halt or diminish job losses. The traditional formula has been: money from the rates, with or without additional private funds, directed to strengthening weak businesses, but also demanding some worker participation in the future running of the plant. In London much more will be done: support and encouragement will be given to workers who, threatened by the dole, are looking for credible alternatives to the dead end of management's profit-based accounting. As Hilary Wainwright has put it, 'The Greater London Council has thrown away the broken compass provided by profit.'

In London it is understood that if socialist planning is to become a reality, people need to be given the resources to do the planning themselves. The process can start without the need for computers, and even *before* the next Labour government takes office, by asking questions like: Why unemployment? Why is this plant 'uncompetitive'? Who says that such and such is 'inefficient'? What alternatives exist to closure? The basis of socialist planning can be laid even under Thatcherism by challenging the seeming inevitability of private decision-making. The real force of the current economic interventions of the GLC is far greater than the £40 million or so that it might spend on the London economy. Its strength lies in the educational process it will have set in motion if enough Londoners become interested in finding their own answers to economic and social decline.

The talk in the Labour Party and TUC about planning institutions the next Labour government might set up is premature. The planning council, national economic assessment, planning ministry and so forth are far less important to socialist planning than they seem. The confidence that people can win by resisting plant closures today is much more important. There is no need to wait for a Labour government to switch on the planning machinery. Indeed, it would be harmful to the socialist planning cause if too much reliance were to be placed (as in the past) on the next Labour government to 'sort it all out'. Socialist planning can only be built on the confidence that working people have in their own ability to run things. Without that confidence throughout the country, capitalist resistance will make short work of any new planning attempt by Labour ministers.

The planning tragedy of the 1970s in the UK was not that Labour's ideas were bankrupt but that the government positively discouraged planning action on the shop floor. It was not enough that there was a Lúcas plan, a plan for Vickers Scotswood or for Tress Engineering, but it might have been a different story if workers in *every* large firm had a socially responsible plan for its development. It is not for any technical reason that more extensive planning would lead to better economic co-ordination. A plan for every major firm is a requirement for *political* reasons. Capitalist resistance to the extension of democracy inherent in socialist planning will only be overcome if workers really do believe that they can make a better job of economic decision-making.

The TUC–Labour Party liaison committee has produced an interesting catalogue of potential planning institutions, but it might be more useful now to look for ways of taking up the fight for jobs at shopfloor level. Admittedly, reasoned argument alone is unlikely to persuade the footsoldiers of Thatcherism in the boardrooms to provide more jobs. But if the questions mentioned earlier were more widely taken up, people would begin to discover that there is nothing inevitable about job losses and plant closures. This is surely the most straightforward way of winning people to the socialist economics of common sense, the common sense that sees unemployment as unnecessary and wasteful.

Summary

Socialist planning is about shifting decision-making power from private to public hands. Experience, particularly that of some British workers in the 1970s, as well as the fledgling initiatives of the GLC in the 1980s, shows that there can be a genuinely democratic socialist planning. Perhaps the most important lesson from planning history is that, fundamentally, planning problems are political and not technical. This holds true for Soviet-type central planning, where difficulties stem basically from the system's lack of democracy. It is also the lesson of Labour's failure to plan in the 1970s, when the hostility of big business saw to it that the state would *not* become an entrepreneur. This lesson is the one that the Labour Party seems least eager to acknowledge. The result is a misplaced belief that the shift in power involved in socialist planning will come about as the result of an almost 'gentlemanly' agreement following the election of a Labour government. On the other hand, if people are well organised and determined, if they really believe in their capacity to plan their own economic futures, then that power can be taken.

A Guide to Reading

Chapter 2

Maurice Dobb gives a readable and short account of traditional central planning and the problems it generates in *Socialist Planning: Some Problems* (Lawrence & Wishart 1970). A critical account of East European post-war economic development by a former planner is Wlodzimierz Brus's *Socialist Ownership and Political Systems* (RKP 1975). Mario Nuti begins to develop an interesting Marxist analysis of central planning in 'The Contradictions of Socialist Economies: A Marxian Interpretation', *The Socialist Register 1979*.

On the historical development of the Soviet economy, Alec Nove's *Economic History of the USSR* (Penguin 1972) is one of the best, reasonably concise accounts.

A useful description of the unfolding of events leading to the birth of Solidarity is given by Neal Ascherson in *The Polish August* (Penguin 1981). *Solidarność: From Gdansk to Military Repression* (International Socialism 1982) is also of interest. A more detailed account of Polish problems can be found in *Policy and Politics in Contemporary Poland: Reform, Failure and Crisis* (Frances Pinter 1982) edited by Jean Woodall.

Chapter 3

Discussion of socialist planning for Britain seems to begin with G.D.H.Cole in the 1930s in *Practical Economics* (Penguin 1937), *The Machinery of Socialist Planning* (The Hogarth Press 1938) and *Plan for a Democratic Britain* (Odhams Press Ltd 1939). *The*

British War Economy (HMSO 1949) by W.K. Hancock and M.M.Gowing gives a good overview of the economic problems Britain faced in waging the second world war.

Over recent years Stuart Holland has had a great impact on the development of planning ideas starting with his *The State as Entrepreneur* (Weidenfeld 1972) and culminating in the widely noted *The Socialist Challenge* (Quartet 1975).

Doug McEachern is well worth reading on the limits to nationalisation policies in British capitalism in his 'Party government and the class interests of capital: conflict over the steel industry 1945–79', *Capital and Class* (summer 1979). Looking particularly at the 1970s, an important idea was signalled in *The National Enterprise Board* (Labour Party 1973) but it had all but disappeared in the Wilson government's 1974 White Paper, *The Regeneration of British Manufacturing* (Cmnd 5710).

Chapter 4

A detailed account of the labour movement's alternative to Thatcherism can be found in *The Alternative Economic Strategy: A Labour Movement Response to the Economic Crisis* (CSE Books 1980). In addition, the Labour Party and TUC have published position documents on the subject as mentioned in the text. *Britain on the Dole: Unemployment and the Socialist Alternative* is a good attempt by the Labour Party to give the ideas a wider hearing in a well produced and cheap pamphlet. A description of what the next Labour government intends as regards planning is given in *Economic Planning and Industrial Democracy: The Framework for Full Employment* published in 1982 and selling then at £1.00. Most of these publications can be obtained direct from the Labour Party at 150 Walworth Road, London SE17.

As the 1970s progressed, three separate workers' reports appeared which make essential reading for anyone concerned with socialist industrial policy. They are: *A Workers' Enquiry into the Motor Industry* (CSE Books 1978); *Crisis in Engineering: Machine Tools Workers Fight for Jobs* (Institute for Workers' Control, Nottingham 1979); and *State Intervention in Industry: A Workers' Enquiry* (Coventry, Liverpool, Newcastle and North Tyneside Trades Councils, Newcastle 1980).

The Lucas Plan is another 'must' and a short summary can be

found in *Lucas: An Alternative Plan* (IWC Pamphlet no 55, Nottingham 1978). The disappointment of Lucas workers with the Labour government is fully revealed in *Democracy versus the Circumlocution Office* (IWC Pamphlet no. 65, Nottingham 1979). The complete Lucas story is told in *The Lucas Plan: A New Trade Unionism in the Making?* (Allison & Busby 1982) by Hilary Wainwright and Dave Elliott.

The account of what happened at Tress was drawn from *The Closure of Tress: A Fairey Story*, a short pamphlet produced at the Tyneside Socialist Centre (115 Westgate Road, Newcastle). Vickers Scotswood was one of the hardest battlegrounds for workers in the 1970s but out of it an alternative economics was beginning to emerge. As a case study of what a practical economics for socialists means it is immensely useful. The details can be found in *Economic Audit on Vickers Scotswood*, available from the Tyneside Socialist Centre.

Chapter 5

Much of the material in this chapter has been drawn from discussion papers and interviews with individuals involved in the London and West Midlands experiments, and material is freely available from the GLC Economic Policy Group (address below). I have drawn on two articles in particular, one by Alan McGarvey, 'Cure for a sick capital', *The Accountant*, 9 December 1982, the other by Hilary Wainwright, 'A socialist GLC in capitalist Britain?', *Capital and Class*, winter 1982, no. 18.

Useful contacts and addresses:

London

'Jobs for a Change' is the slogan that sums up what the Economic Policy Group at the Greater London Council is about. Further information is available from the EPG at Room 6b, The County Hall, SE1 (tel 01-633 5959). Educational material explaining 'popular planning' is being produced by the Popular Planning Unit at County Hall (tel 01-633 5958). A Project Development Unit has also been set up by the policy group to go out to workplace and community groups to help shape ideas for employment projects. It is in Room 8 at the County Hall (tel 01-633 1490. The Greater London Enterprise Board can be contacted through the EPG.

The 'Jobs from Warmth' group can be reached at The Thornhill

Neighbourhood Project, Orkney House, 199 Caledonian Road, Islington (tel 01-278 9500).

West Midlands

Information on the council's economic policies can be obtained from the Economic Development Unit, West Midlands County Council, County Hall, Birmingham. The West Midlands Enterprise Board is located at 75 Edmund Street, Birmingham.

The best known trade union and community research centre in the West Midlands is Coventry Workshop at 40 Binley Road, Coventry (tel 0203-27772).

Elsewhere

Details of Sheffield's economic policy are available from its Employment Committee, Town Hall, Sheffield (tel 0742-734118). Other local trade union and community research centres include: Bradford Resource Centre, 93–95 Little Horton Lane, Bradford (tel 0274-25046); Bristol Resource Centre, 82 Bedminster Parade, Bristol (tel 0272-667933); Leeds Trade Union and Community Research Centre, 6 Blenheim Terrace, Leeds (tel 0532-39633); West End Resource Centre, 87 Adelaide Terrace, Benwell, Newcastle-upon-Tyne (tel 0632-732943/731210); Tyne and Wear Resource Centre, 2 Jesmond Road, Newcastle-upon-Tyne (tel 0632-811911); 118 Workshop, 118 Mansfield Road, Nottingham (tel 0602-582369).